273

The Hitchhiking Years
and Four Other Stories

Don White

has produced

Ten CDs

Three live concert DVDs

This is his second book.

www.DonWhite.net

The Hitchhiking Years and Four Other Stories

by

Don White

Barry Park Press
Lynn, Massachusetts

First printing October 2021

Edited by Terence Hegarty
Cover art and design by Ann Marie Catabia
Front photo by Skip Bowes
Back photo by Mark Steele

Contact: www.DonWhite.net

ISBN 978-0-9969921-9-0

Printed in the United States of America
By King Printing Co., Inc. Lowell, Massachusetts

This book is dedicated to Theresa White

Contents

Foreword

Fifteen years ago, when I finished my first collection of short stories (*Memoirs of a C Student*), I said I'd never write another book. I meant it. But since fifty is the new thirty, I'm making the case that in years between books, fifteen is the new never.

A man who willfully chose to spend his working years as an alarm installer, a folksinger, and a storyteller should not be surprised when in his golden years these noble endeavors fail to meet his fiscal retirement needs.

I wrote this book because I needed the money. That doesn't mean I didn't enjoy it. It means my financial realities and my dearth of options in that arena created a compelling argument for its creation.

There are five stories here. The one about my dad and the hitchhiking one are both true—whatever that means. With the three others I freed myself from the tyranny of truth-telling. I created characters by melding together the personalities and idiosyncrasies of different people I have met to fit the needs of the stories I wanted to tell. It was exhilarating. Writing fiction, it turns out, is a freeing and enjoyable enterprise.

By 2020 I had written four stories—approximately half a

book. Then good old Covid 19 showed up and was kind enough to grant me the two things I needed to finish the other half: The inability to earn money via the shutting down of performance venues, and the gobs of free time that new reality so considerately bestowed upon my world.

That's when the stories from the three years I spent hitchhiking around North America with my then girlfriend and now wife submitted their applications for the job. They had done so many times in the past and were always denied because they couldn't or wouldn't answer the one crucial question: What is the story?

I would rather go broke than write a glorified blog on being a hitchhiker. "Got a ride by some freaks in a van in Albuquerque. They had killer weed—a trucker drove us all the way to San Francisco—the cops hassled us in Kansas."

But I needed the money and I needed the pages. After much reflection a story worthy of consideration emerged. It was about America in the mid-seventies and a method of travel that is lost to history—a story of uncompromised freedom—of how the road opened our world to unlimited possibilities and ... it is a love story.

For several months now I have been getting up at five o'clock in the morning to write about these adventures. I do so until my eyeballs hurt and my mind has turned to mush. That's a lot of time to be thinking about the extraordinary early years of my long history with the blue-eyed, raven-haired, free-spirited, modern-day pioneer woman of my dreams. At some point the process began to reignite the part of my brain where high-voltage youthful romance once burned. One day, after yet another eight hours of writing about the formative early years of our relationship, I emerged from my office. I sat beside my wife on the couch and gave her a long kiss. It freaked her out. She was sure I'd gone over the edge.

So go ahead and start reading the book. I hope you enjoy it. My pioneer woman is working on a computer in the living room. While you're learning about who we were and the adventures we had back when an outstretched thumb was our vehicle for escaping the life we had known and discovering the unlimited possibilities of who we could become, I'm going to go ask her if she wants to kiss me like she did when we were eighteen and sleeping under the stars beside the AlCan Highway in the Yukon Territory with nothing to think about except spontaneity and adventure.

The Hitchhiking Years
and Four Other Stories

THE HITCHHIKING YEARS

Part 1

Selling Our House

My wife and I make sounds now when we rise from the sitting position. These quasi-moans and other primal emissions are akin to those that might emanate from the throats of slightly wounded animals.

We went out for coffee this morning. If you were near our driveway when we returned, our slow and cautious emergence from the car and our involuntary audio would have left little doubt that you were observing what is commonly known as an elderly couple.

The brain behind a pair of eyes translates what those eyes see in accordance with its ability and willingness to think. It is perfectly reasonable for a passerby, after a cursory glance, to think of Mrs. White as a gray-haired woman in need of a knee replacement. That would be an accurate, albeit lazy, assessment.

To these eyes that now peer out from beneath brows of gray she is forever nineteen. They see the now world-seasoned Mrs. White in the flower dress that she bought for fifty cents in a flea market in Arizona with the desert wind flirtatiously mussing her long black hair. We were a few months into the first of three separate years of hitchhiking adventures around North America in the nineteen seventies. I was then and am now hopelessly smitten by this woman to the point where my brain has permanently beguiled my eyes.

For the past thirty years we have lived in a house that is within walking distance from where we each grew up. We just spent thirteen thousand dollars to take this 1910 gem of a cottage from lived-in to showable. The kitchen looks nice—new floor, new windows, new ceiling and walls.

The house is for sale. Our recollections of all that transpired here in the past three decades are not. They are packed neatly into our memories in taped and magic-markered boxes.

There's no getting around the fact that this should be a moment of reflection. Within these walls we fulfilled our biological obligation to propagate the species. The kids are grown. My parents are dead. Our grandchildren are older now than their parents were when we moved here. As definitive proof that I fear no tired football metaphor, I offer this: there is no one blocking downfield for us. It's a straight shot to the end zone for her and me.

I could/should be thinking about the odds I beat to go from non-college, unskilled laborer to building a fulfilling career— how in 1973 the smart money would have been on me dying, or at least having my potential significantly diminished by drugs and alcohol—how we never missed a house payment, raised kids that function well in a complex world, and how I am still hopelessly in love with the girl I did all that adventuring with. This moment is demanding that I reflect upon and indulge these accomplishments. But I can't. I just keep thinking about hippies.

Hybrid

My career as a songwriter/storyteller has benefitted immeasurably from the songs and stories I created about parenting teenagers. For a while it seemed like the subject would provide me an inexhaustible amount of quality material. Here are a few takeaways from the experience that have been tempered by time and the luxury of being able to see the kind of adults my teenagers grew to be.

Are your teenagers driving you nuts? Good. That's what they're built for. If you have a teenager that doesn't rebel against you, take him or her to a doctor because their inability to execute their primary function is damaged and in urgent need of repair. "Doctor, please help us. This teenager is nice. We try our best but she just won't rebel. She won't sneak out at night. She won't say she hates us. We leave whiskey in an unlocked cabinet and she won't drink it and replace what she has taken with water. We feel we've failed as parents. What ever shall we do?"

All right. That's enough of that. I don't think improv comedy riffing is going to help make this chapter a more enjoyable experience for the reader.

I want to talk about the disproportionate effect that experiences engender within the unhardened cement of one's personality when they occur during adolescence.

But first, here is the only piece of information that I learned during my years on the peculiar and annoying battlefield of teenager-raising that I can still offer with confidence.

The garden analogy.

The only thing you can be sure about your garden is that if you don't water it nothing will grow. Conversely, all the water and care in the world won't guarantee a harvest. And most importantly, if you do tend your garden well and are blessed with a harvest it will not arrive till autumn. It is a special kind of foolish to expect full-grown tomatoes to appear while you are watering tomato seeds.

Picture this scenario. Your teenager does or says something so stupid that you begin to wonder if you might be dreaming. You pinch yourself, yelp, and succumb to the unfortunate fact that the situation before you is actually happening. You then patiently, methodically, and with great love and care, explain in detail all the verifiable reasons why said teenager's current behavior or view is insane and if practiced in the real world will terminate in a probation office at best or a casket at worst.

Now imagine that your teenager looks you in the eye and says, "You know, I never really thought of it that way. Thank you so much for helping me to understand how wrong I was and how foolish my thinking on this matter has been. I am so grateful to you for taking the time to set me straight. As of this moment I am going to change who I am. I shall turn a new leaf, abandon my prior view and wholeheartedly adopt and implement the philosophy that you have so caringly explained. And never shall I return to the reckless worldview that your lecture has so meticulously deconstructed."

I believe that if you ever heard these words from a teenager that they would be marinated in sarcasm.

Water them. Keep them in the sun, and hope for a good harvest in the fall.

That's all I've got. Hope it helps.

*****

When I was a teenager and the adult I was going to become was being shaped by the times and my early interests, hippies ruled the world—at least the part of it that drew and held my attention. The release of the Woodstock album and movie—

peace rallies—love-ins. I saw hippies every night on the news putting flowers into the rifles of riot police, protesting the war, tripping out of their skulls and dancing in Golden Gate Park. If one was to believe the news reports, and why wouldn't one, they were everywhere. I wanted to be a hippie. I was born for it. But the stork was drunk and instead of delivering me to my rightful destination in Haight Ashbury, he dropped me into a hippieless, incurably blue-collar East Coast factory town called Lynn, Massachusetts.

During my impressionable teenage years the stretch of Western Avenue from McDonough Square to Breed Square in my fair city was referred to as Hippie Haven. It should have been called Get-Wasted-and-Pass-Out-on-the-Sidewalk Haven. There were lots of long-haired people milling around in front of the Dunkin' Donuts but even at fifteen I knew they weren't hippies. There was no peace and love happening there ... none. As far as I could see it was an outdoor dispensary for drugs—primarily barbiturates.

There have been countless documentaries of the crack and heroin epidemics but what about those years when barbs were king? Now that was a documentary-worthy time if ever a time there was. In those days doctors were handing out the stuff without constraint. Every third medicine cabinet you opened had a prescription bottle full of seconal, nembutal, reds or quaaludes. What happened to those drugs? I bet it's been twenty years since I heard a person even speak their names.

In the movie *The Wolf of Wall Street*, Leonardo DiCaprio does a superb job showing what a person wasted on quaaludes looks like. Watch it. Then picture a two-block area filled with people on ludes. It was unreal. Heaps of drooling, mumbling people lying on top of each other reaching out a hand and making guttural sounds as you walk by. It was as if via pre-language communication they were begging you to save them from some post-apocalyptic version of barbiturate hell. There is no present-day equivalent—I would ask those of you familiar enough with the current heroin epidemic to be able to visualize a neighborhood of users stoned enough to nod off and drown in their bowls of soup, to multiply the degree of intoxication in that scene by a factor of twenty. The neighborhood between McDonough and Breed Square during the barbiturate era of the early nineteen seventies was populated by young people in a state of intoxication that would by comparison make a heroin user seem downright perky. If I had not lived in that place in those times I really wouldn't believe it.

Long hair? Yes. But not one other thing did these fleshy mumbling piles of lost humanity have in common with hippies. Were it not for news reports from San Francisco, I would have had no idea that the peace and love thing existed. The long-haired people in my world were wasted and wounded and thinking (when thinking was possible) about things of a much more primal nature.

One summer day I was with some friends alongside our local reservoir. We were enjoying the finished product of a mixture of malted barley, hops, yeast and water that a noble brew master, whom we didn't know but held in great esteem, had painstakingly melded and sealed inside the keg we had carried with loving care from the car. Our appreciation ceremony had been under way for nary an hour when two smartly uniformed policemen inserted themselves into the revelry and unceremoniously escorted us from the area. They did let us keep the beer. (Much to the amazement of the guy whose house we parked near as he watched the cops let us place the keg in the trunk.) Ah, the seventies, no mothers against drunk driving, just "get outta my neighborhood with that beer you punks."

We wound up in a patch of woods behind some apartment buildings. We smoked and drank there for six or seven hours. Some of the long-haired not hippies who hung around Not Hippie Haven showed up as soon as we arrived. (They had an infallible, fine-tuned radar for finding free beer gatherings.)

That night when the beer and weed were gone and we were getting ready to leave, my friend walked up to me and said, "Joey has been passed out in those bushes for hours." [Nothing unusual about seeing that from one of these older guys.] "I just tried to wake him up so he wouldn't spend the night here and … he's cold." "Here, give him my sweatshirt," says I. "No," says he, "not cold like he needs a blanket but cold like maybe dead."

One of the older guys who was just back from Vietnam pressed his fingers against Joey's neck and felt his wrist for a pulse. Sure enough, Joey was not only dead but had been so for enough hours that when his friends were putting him in their Volkswagen beetle to transport his remains to the hospital, it took a bit of effort to bend him into it.

In 2019, Lynn was one of the top ten cities for fatal overdoses in Massachusetts. I'm sure that with the easy availability of barbiturates and with heroin coming in from Vietnam, my hometown was in the top ten in the early seventies as well. To many people who live in more affluent places these fatalities are just statistics. To us they are people we went to school with— people we know and love—human beings who had just as much potential to do something great in the world as anyone else.

On the walls of the home of Joey's parents were photographs of him playing baseball and graduating from high school and laughing with his siblings. It is infuriating to those of us who live with the scourge of substance abuse to see these friends and family members reduced to data points and stripped of their humanity.

When I was seventeen years old, death by drugs and alcohol via overdose or car crash was an all too frequent occurrence in my community of friends. Each time it happened, I imagined my mother staring at my Little League trophies and knowing that luck and the right decision at a key moment was all that separated me from the exact same fate.

I was living an extremely high-risk existence. An abrupt and tragic end was certainly possible. I knew I had to get away.

A few months later I was hitchhiking around North America with my girlfriend. We met more real peace and love hippies than we could count. The west coast of the country was overrun with them. But even the ocean-less, mountain-less, so-this-is-where-they-grow-wheat middle of the country states almost always had a college town where we could follow the smell of patchouli and incense past their regional version of conventional America to where dorm room turntables were spinning The Grateful Dead and transient members of the tribe were always welcome to roll their sleeping bags out on the floor.

I immersed myself in the culture. But every time we got picked up by a flower child in a VW, I knew that I was the only person the driver would ever meet who once saw the body of an overdose victim bent into one and that my life experience would never permit me to embrace the kind of naiveté necessary to be a true peace and love hippie. I would have to settle for becoming something of a hybrid.

The Place I Was Leaving

Well-rested, hydrated, nutritioned and gently caffeinated Don White at Lynn beach:

I could never live away from the ocean. The sound and feel of the waves breaking on the beach is in my blood. This same water carried my ancestors to a new world where, with nothing but determination, they built a life the foundation of which would benefit their descendants in ways they would not live to see.

I love this place. Watching first-generation families splashing in these waters en route to the American dream to the sound-track of waves against the seawall touches a place of hope in me that has its origins in the dreams of my forefathers (and fore-mothers).

Sleep-deprived, dehydrated, sugar-donut-for-breakfast, ten-cups-of-coffee-before-noon Don White at Lynn Beach:

This place looks and smells like a sewer! While breathing in the rancid stench as the brown waves break in sadness on this tragic beach, a person might justifiably hypothesize that a four-hundred-ton pterodactyl with a severe case of explosive diarrhea un-loaded here while flying by.

And everybody just walks by like it's normal. It is not normal! Tell you what, if this crap was stinking up shorefront million-dollar homes in Swampscott, Marblehead or Nahant you can bet your ass that all hell would break loose until the source was found, a remedy was applied, and home values of the affluent were protected. But because this disgusting mess is contained on one section of Lynn beach—nothing. Just "get used to it" like we do with all the other bullshit that happens here that none of the towns with money ever have to deal with.

It's not just the water here that stinks. The attitude of so many of the locals—both newly arrived and multigenerational—smells just as bad. Here ... look at this. Some family spent the day on this section of sand on the Nahant side of the beach where the water isn't brown. At the end of the day they took their kids and left everything else—empty bottles, half-eaten sandwiches, plastic wrappers, empty cardboard boxes and four ... count 'em ... four used disposable diapers. The level of not-giving-a-shit-about-anybody-or-anything that we are subjected to daily in this city is oppressive and relentless.

As you can see, dear reader, the way I feel about my hometown depends entirely on the amount of sleep I got the night before and the levels of water, nourishment and caffeine that my body contains.

*****

The summer after I graduated from high school my dad got me a job on the line crew working for the city. My boss was an old alcoholic and lifelong Lynner named Mickey. He was a year away from retirement and had worked for the city his entire adult life.

What a gig that was in those days. There was almost no rule you could break that could get you fired. The good old boy network that ran this place could and would quash any challenge to your job security with an ease that spoke volumes about their invincibility. There was no such thing as a cell phone video, accountability was unheard of, and the local power structure was the constant beneficiary of a community newspaper with a see-no-evil attitude.

Our job was to repair and replace electrical lines throughout the city. Every day while we were unloading wire from the bucket truck Mickey would disappear and return within three minutes.

At that time Lynn was a town with more neighborhood bars per capita than any of the surrounding communities. Mickey, through years of focused determination, had trained every bartender who worked a day shift in the city to start pouring a shot of Old Tom at the instant he opened the door. In less than thirty seconds our enterprising crew chief would slide the contents of the shot glass down his throat while simultaneously placing the price of the drink plus a healthy tip's worth of prefolded cash on the bar and be on his way back to the work site.

If utilizing an entire city's network of daytime bartenders to maintain a steady flow of alcohol to one's blood stream while being paid a handsome wage were an Olympic event, this old Lynner would be the gold medal champion. I have often imagined the utopian paradise this world might have known if the decades of time and energy Mickey spent on making sure that he was never more than three minutes away from a drink had instead been devoted to eliminating world poverty.

By afternoon, after he had imbibed a certain quantity of Old Tom, Mickey would become quiet. His answers to your questions would be delayed a few seconds because his brain had shifted to the sort of functioning alcoholic auto pilot that one becomes accustomed to seeing with this particular type of Olympian. But in the morning when we were gathered at the shop he was chatty and always anxious to enlighten me with unsolicited pearls of his own unique brand of working-class wisdom.

"Maughnin' kid. You look tired. Were you out chasin' the broads last night? You'll never get to heaven that way you know." The other three men on the crew looked up from their respective newspapers, their faces betraying the mischief beneath their attempts to appear earnest as they nodded in agreement. Then

Mickey (self-proclaimed line crew spiritual advisor) said, "theah is only one way for guys like us to get those pearly gates to open." "Clean living!" shouted his disciples in unison before folding their papers, draining the coffee from styrofoam cups, and rising from the table to attend to the electrical needs of our humble village.

I sat beside Mickey that morning in the front seat of the bucket truck. "I been thinkin' about you," said he. "We all ahh lucky to be on this crew because we nevah have to work directly with the public. We just pull wiahs, hook 'em up and go home. But you, with your fathah's connections, might wind up workin' at City Hall or in some job wheah you would have to interact face to face with Mr. and Mrs. John Q. Public. Heeah's what you need to know. Bein' a kid from Lynn, whenevah someone tells you that they don't like the work you did or they want you to do it theiah way instead, it's gonna be natural for you to tell them to stuff their opinions up their ass. But I gotta tell ya, that won't fly with the general public. You probably think that everybody out theah has the same kinda attitude as people from Lynn but they don't. Getting told by a workin' guy to stuff it up your ass is going to be a brand new experience for your average woman from Nahant. It'll piss her off royally and she'll be on the phone in two minutes tryna git you fired. I know, it's haahd to believe but it's true. So, heah's my advice for you kid. When one of these rich women stahts talkin' to you like you're the dog who chewed up her shoes, no mattah how much you want to and no mattah how much she deserves to heah it, you cannot tell her to stuff it up her ass. This is what you do. You pause for a minute, put ya fingah to ya chin like the bullshit she just said was actually worth thinkin' about and then, in a calm voice you say, 'I'll get back to you on that.'" Then the old, alcoholic, dispenser of proletarian wisdom put his arm around me and said, "It means the same thing."

Leaving Home

Reflecting upon the prelaunch period of my hitchhiking years, I am fascinated by my spectacularly comprehensive unpreparedness. The definitive encapsulating example being the moment I realized that having "planned" a route that would take me down the coast of America's northwest I neglected to anticipate that it might possibly rain. I never gave it a thought until the Japanese current decided to educate me to the fact that the mosses on all the trees near the ocean in Washington state were the beneficiaries of the 38 inches of rain that falls for an average of one hundred and fifty-six days a year.

Picture me standing alongside Interstate 5 near Seattle in the pouring rain wearing a green trash bag that I had frantically torn holes in to accommodate my head and arms after coming to terms with the fact that I failed to bring rain gear on what I hoped would be a years-long hitchhiking adventure.

Your answer to the following question will provide a nice touchstone for how different the world has become since the year of our lord nineteen hundred and seventy-four. "Do you know a single living person today who would give one moment of consideration to picking up a hitchhiker wearing a trash bag?"

The road wanted to change me. It wanted to expand my world and unleash my potential. But it had to bring a hefty quantity of patience to the endeavor. The person within which it hoped to stimulate an evolutionary spark was viscerally dispositioned to defending the status quo against all threats foreign and domestic.

During the first months following my departure from the only life I had known I was ensconced in a hermetically sealed traveling bubble of Lynnness. I basically just took my partying show on the road—drinking all night in the club car from Montreal to Vancouver on the Trans Canada Railway, partying all night with teenagers that picked me up in Oregon, nestling in, and you guessed it, partying, with a group of Lynners who were sequestered in an apartment in San Francisco and so on.

In the book *Travels with Charley* Steinbeck wrote, "When we get these thruways across the whole country, as we will and must, it will be possible to drive from New York to California without seeing a single thing."

I would argue that a narrow frame of mind, a lack of curiosity, or an inability to be in the moment will invisible-ize what is in front of you with an attention to detail that the interstate highway system could only dream of. "Get outta my way Rocky Mountains. I gotta get to California to partaay!"

During my first few months away from home I was in an impenetrable no-growth zone. I behaved in the manner to which I had grown accustomed from the age of fourteen or so.

Let's start the story in late 1974 in Tucson, Arizona. Being near the border of Mexico, Tucson is a very attractive destination for those vacationers whose extended holiday plans struggle under the weight of impoverishment. In winter, along with visitors of affluence, the town is besieged by the type of traveler for whom indoor plumbing would be considered an extravagance. The city's proximity to the equator relative to the rest of North America suggested to me (and to a colorful assortment of hitchhikers, vagabonds, ne'er-do-wells, and the chronically unemployable) that sleeping in the desert outside of town would be heavenly.

It wasn't. It was cold. I woke up every morning with ice on my sleeping bag. I just now googled "why are deserts cold at night?" It turns out that there is a simple scientific explanation. Of course, in 1974 Google was just the dream of a newborn nerd and was coincidently inaccessible to me. I woke up every morning shivering and bemoaning the unfairness of the situation and demanding that deserts acquiesce to my impregnable under-standing of how they should behave.

I shoplifted a bit. I washed up as best I could in restaurant and gas station bathrooms. I hitchhiked up and down Speedway Boulevard in the evening until someone picked me up and got me stoned (which happened every evening.) Then I slept outside of town between two mesquite bushes as happy as a clam—a clam with inexplicable ice on his sleeping bag in the morning, but happy nonetheless.

The Kindness of Strangers

Most people I knew who hitchhiked in those days wound up getting a job somewhere. Not me. Jobs embodied the kind of subservience and life of quiet desperation that I was determined to evade for as long as possible. In the rearview mirror of the car that drove me away from my hometown I distinctly remember seeing the outstretched tentacles of long-term gainful employment beckoning me to reconsider and reminding me that I could run but I could not hide from their patient and determined grasp.

I had saved eleven hundred dollars from my summer lineman job. I took two hundred in traveler's cheques and left the rest with my mother to dispense to me in small amounts as needed.

I had no idea how this adventure would unfold or terminate but I knew for sure that running out of money would send out a homing beacon to the long bony fingers of the working world and trigger an abrupt and perhaps permanent termination to my adventuring. I also knew with a visceral and unequivocable certainty that if eleven hundred dollars were in my pocket I could and would party it away in a month.

Maybe it was the times. Maybe it was naiveté. Maybe it was

drug-induced brain damage, but even with no life experiences to use as reference I had a persistent gut feeling that most strangers would be kind to me. I was right. So right in fact that barely a month into being a fulltime ride solicitor I had extrapolated from a few timely dispensed kindnesses that the generosity *of* strangers *to* strangers, while not guaranteed, occurred frequently enough to be considered a reasonably reliable eventuality.

I received the first significant validation of my unsubstantiated assumption when I caught a ride from Jim Powers. He pulled over in his three-speed Ford Falcon and asked me where I was going. I said, "to the outskirts of town to sleep on the ground." To which he replied that I was "welcome to stay at his house."

I can feel you tightening up after reading that last sentence. Relax. Yes, I was seventeen years old and living within an impenetrable cloud of cluelessness. However, within the context of deciding if someone posed a threat to my well-being, my proficiency, even at that time, was impressive. Previous generations of Lynners who failed to develop this skill set never lived long enough to reproduce. You can't find one of us now who doesn't excel in this field. It's a fundamental survival skill—not infallible of course, but consistently reliable. And Jim made it easy. He was a really good guy and I knew it instantly.

We became quick friends. He told me I could stay as long as I wanted. I may have paid him some small amount toward his rent but it's just as likely that he let me live there for free. Between 1974 and 1979 I was always welcome to stay with him.

I've tried unsuccessfully to find him online in the past few years. I feel like I never adequately thanked him for all he did for me. I've changed his name here to one that rhymes with his actual name so if he's still among the living maybe he'll get to read the following belated words of gratitude. SB, my appreciation for your kindness and generosity and your patience and understanding has grown exponentially as the decades have passed. Today, with the eyes of a fully grown man, I see how your friendship and your giving nature gave me the opportunity to alter the trajectory of my life and eventually become the person I hoped to be. Thank you.

Theresa

Many self-proclaimed happily married people are incapable of stopping themselves from telling anyone that will listen about how much deeper and more fulfilling love is when it is has had enough time to properly season.

You might naively have assumed that the response from one of these folks to a question you innocently posed about lawn care would not initiate a well-worn dissertation on the wonderfulness of old love versus the shallowness of new love. You may also have experienced a moment of bewilderment when that lecture veered off into a detailed list of the many poems, songs, and novels dedicated to revealing the lack of depth in young love while extolling the countless benefits of the more seasoned variety.

Although the recipients of this unsolicited information might understandably have hoped that its impartation could be, shall we say, a bit less condescending and interminable, they are obliged to acknowledge that the truth at the heart of the message is beyond reproach.

Every one of those songs, stories, and poems reveals an unimpeachable truth. There is no comparison between the depth of love between two humans that have worked together to build a new life and raise a family and two who have not. There. I said it. I mean it. I am officially and permanently on record as being in total agreement.

But remembering that I fully concur with the unassailable assessment that old love is the greatest, might I, just for the sake of argument, and not in any way to diminish the sovereignty of old love, say, gently and with all due respect, that the one thing, and it's only one single thing, that might be put in the plus column for young love, that old love, again, with all due respect, doesn't have is ... VOLTAGE.

One summer night I was standing with a group of my neighbors across the street from a car that had knocked down a telephone pole. There were electrical wires lying everywhere. During our community gawking session one of those wires shifted and when the live end touched the metal of the car roof a giant blue arc lit up the night with a popping/cracking sound that was so loud it made everyone within 200 feet jump back and yelp.

When I realized at seventeen years old that Theresa McDermott might possibly be at least slightly attracted to me I felt like my body was hooked up to that downed wire and it was delivering its high voltage blue arc of light and that electrical explosion directly into my bloodstream. The thought of seeing her, kissing her, and ... oh man ... touching her, electrified me to the point where I'm certain that whenever I thought of her my head would begin to smell like overheated circuitry.

How I felt at the moment she appeared at the door of Jim's house in Tucson is entirely beyond my ability to describe. Suffice it to say that was the day my life as I have come to know it began. Some ancient inaccessible part of me knew this and responded by unleashing a year's worth of dopamine to my brain's pleasure centers. If you could see the smile on my face now as I recall that moment, my countenance would articulate to you what I was feeling much more eloquently than any words I could assemble.

Six weeks after leaving home I had a place to stay, the girl of my dreams by my side, and a world of unlimited and unpredictable adventure awaiting our imminent disembarkation from the stifling safety of stability.

*****

It was a very pleasant 65 degrees on the Ides of March when Theresa and I packed up our ample misconceptions and left Tucson for the first time to visit the Grand Canyon. Via some unresearched postulations and a lack of appreciation for the benefits of due diligence, we assumed that the entire state of Arizona would be similarly temperatured.

We carried a pop tent with us that had a mosquito net top which we secured a tarp over in the event that we encountered any of that balmy Arizona rain.

I'd like to take this opportunity to thank the Grand Canyon for being kind enough to teach us three important things that had an immediate impact on our ability to stay alive and out of jail in our future travels.

1) That it is a good thing to have sleeping bags that zip together and a warm body to spoon with after you set up your screen-covered pop tent on the ridge of the canyon in three inches of snow.

2) It's the elevation stupid. The closer you are to the moon the colder it will be no matter what state you are in. (A lesson we would relearn to the extreme in June when the t-shirt weather at the base of the Rocky Mountains failed to inform us of the fourteen feet of snow at the top of the pass.)

3) National forests are a better destination for vagabonds than national parks for several reasons having to do with the number and type of tourists that frequent each but mostly because of regulations and how many rangers are employed to enforce them.

(While we were shivering in our tent on top of the ridge the police swooped in and hauled away the folks in the camp beside us for smoking weed. After that, with very few exceptions, we avoided national parks.)

SNACK Sunday

After becoming educated about the lack of concern that higher elevations had for the body temperatures of exposed humans, Theresa and I practiced and developed our hitchhiking skills by traveling back and forth between Tucson and San Francisco. It was an 866-mile run that featured friends with a floor we could sleep on at each end with a conspicuous absence of altitude in between.

For us these trips were akin to learning to ride a bike with training wheels. There was so much to learn and, as surprising as it might seem, there were no hitchhiking manuals available for purchase at that time. It seems like a monumental failure of the free enterprise system that no one created a *Hitchhiking for Dummies* handbook to capitalize on the era's burgeoning market. But on second thought, I imagine that the proposal may have been tabled after it was suggested during the pitch meeting that the target audience would be largely inclined to shoplift the product. So, we reassessed what worked and what didn't after each of these relatively short excursions.

Those early days were marked by eighteen-year-old exuberance. We travelled all night. We didn't need sleep. We needed movement. Destinations existed for a cursory glance and a good night's sleep between what would otherwise be a life of perpetual motion.

In late March of 1975 legendary concert promoter Bill Graham put together a benefit event at Kesar Stadium in San Francisco called SNACK Sunday. It was to feature the Grateful

Dead, Santana, Jefferson Starship, The Doobie Brothers, Joan Baez, Neil Young, and Tower of Power. It was rumored that Bob Dylan might show up.

We learned about the show two days before it was to happen. You know, no internet, no cell phones and no algorithms making sure that you always know where to spend your money via customized advertisements that data mining enabled your corporate overlords to create in order to serve their (I mean, your) needs.

We read about it in a discarded underground music magazine that we picked up off the sidewalk on Fourth Avenue in Tucson.

Seconds after reading about the concert and with the magazine still in my hand I said to Theresa, "If we leave today, we might make it there just before the gates open." "Cool. Let's go" was her reply.

If you want to know the primary reason why we got hopelessly addicted to hitchhiking even though we were often sleeping under bridges alongside humans of questionable character, alternately sun-baked and rain-soaked, at the mercy of strangers and occasionally a bit malnourished, ask yourself this question. Could I put this book down, pack a bag and go wherever I choose for as long as I want right now?

I wasn't sure that I fully understood anything about the world except that it was not designed to encourage and facilitate unadulterated spontaneity. And the more I grew to appreciate how few people would ever experience a week of that, let alone the years I intended to devote, it became impossible for me to imagine a difficulty or challenge that wouldn't be worth enduring and learning to overcome as long as it served to sustain my access to more obstinate, impulsive, unfettered freedom.

We arrived at Kesar Stadium on Sunday morning an hour before the concert was due to start. We had hitchhiked for over twenty-four hours straight. The next day, during our post-journey assessment meeting, an extensive list of high-risk behaviors was brought before the board. A motion to abstain from said behaviors during any and all future excursions in perpetuity was proposed. It passed unanimously and was summarily written into the bylaws.

In the three hundred and seventy-three miles between Phoenix and Los Angeles lies more nothing than the mind of a native New Englander is equipped to comprehend. It's a Zen master's dream. Nothing but nothing and then a great big bunch of more nothing.

Placed inexplicably between miles of desert to the east and west is Indio, California. Ever heard of it? Probably not. But anyone who ever hitched from LA to Arizona will probably have a story to tell about this desert town, and more specifically for the purposes of this tale, her long lonesome on-ramp to Interstate 10.

In the three years that I spent on the road I travelled the LA-Phoenix highway no less than fifteen times. Only once was I able to avoid a lengthy layover on this legendary ramp.

Because the NO PEDESTRIANS ON THE INTERSTATE law was strictly enforced at that time in California, the Indio on-ramp was an unavoidable catch basin, involuntary gathering spot, mid-desert dehydration center, and (we often conjectured) the final resting place for the sun-bleached bones of past strandees.

It's a long straight ramp designed, one would imagine, so that automobiles would be traveling at sixty-five miles per hour when they merged on to the highway. I'd prefer to think that the designers were thoughtful enough to take into consideration that of all the on-ramps in the United States this one would need extra length to accommodate the country's largest population of marooned transients.

Hitchhiker etiquette, if there is such a thing, dictates that the person at the beginning of the ramp has been there the longest and is the rightful occupant of that prime real estate. Being knowledgeable and well-mannered members of this traveling community of vagrants, we walked past individuals and pairs of vagabonds in varying stages of sunstroke.

The light pole that we leaned our backpacks against was covered with poetry, witticisms, sketches, and the last wills and testaments of previous visitors. I was thinking about what great pearls of wisdom I might contribute to this living monument to life on the road and preparing for another long stay when the first car we saw, after driving past the desperate outstretched thumbs and pleading countenances of everyone else, pulled over and let us in. Why? Come on, you know why. Because Theresa was the only female on the ramp. Hitchhiking with a woman creates a lengthy list of challenges. But moments like this, when a driver is trying to decide which of the current Indio on-ramp characters look the safest, the value of the hippie girl in the summer dress cannot be overstated.

Onward to Los Angeles where we got dropped off on a ramp in one of the many industrial, smoggy, noisy, shitty corners of this deceptively monikered "city of angels." After a long, noisy, and entirely unpleasant wait, an *actual* angel delivered us from evil and deposited us outside the city limits.

Onward, onward! Going to see The Dead and ... Dylan!

Saturday night around midnight is where it got interesting. (If by interesting I mean stupid, which I do.)

Every car that ever opened its doors to us was a rolling encapsulation of the life of the driver at that unique moment in time. It's as if the novel of a person's life would open to a page in the middle and Theresa and I were inserted into the narrative for a short chapter and then abruptly and permanently removed from the rest of the story.

One time we got a ride from a man who had been driving back and forth on the main road of his little town for hours. He was very upset and obsessing over a series of injustices that had been perpetrated against him by people with whom he was very close. It was the kind of problem that is unique to life in a small town. He needed to tell someone how disrespected and hurt he felt but everyone he knew was either directly involved or connected to one of the offending scoundrels and he knew that expressing his feelings to any of them would only exacerbate the situation.

So, because God has nothing better to do than to insert himself into the problems of a small-town guy in a pickup truck, he delivered two teenage vagabonds to this isolated corner of the world to ease his suffering.

Our new chauffeur drove us as far as it took to tell us the whole story. We listened attentively. We agreed wholeheartedly that he had been unfairly treated. We empathized and were genuinely outraged at the stunning disrespect he had endured from folks he thought were his friends.

When he let us out, he looked like a completely different person than the one who had picked us up an hour earlier. We were grateful to be of some small service to a stranger in need and also, as one might imagine, for the long ride.

We set up our tent that night behind some bushes that concealed us from the road. While we were lying together with our elbows on the floor of the tent and our heads propped up inches from each other cupped in our open palms we started working on the advertising campaign for our traveling therapy service. "Can't afford a psychiatrist? Pick up hitchhikers and certified therapists Don and Theresa. Pour your heart out. Tell them about your feelings. They will listen nonjudgmentally. You'll feel better and the people you are upset with will never know what you really think about them. And … after you've gotten everything off your chest you can boot them out the car door. They will carry away all your harsh words and hurt feelings and you will never lay eyes on them again … all for the low, low price of a ride to the outskirts of town."

The page of the novel we were inserted into at two o'clock in the morning on this all-night gotta-get-there, gotta-get-there, just-gotta-get-to-the-concert trip, provided us a view into a world that we were never exposed to again. Because … although hitchhiking is by nature an occupation not suitable for the risk-averse, doing it on a weekend between midnight and sunrise, when behind the wheel of most every car on the road are people in varying degrees of reckless abandon, although exciting, is like poking the devil in the eye and daring him to show you what he's made of. Upon reflection we agreed that the amount of dumb luck necessary to survive a repeat performance of the journey I am about to describe was more than anyone could reasonably expect to have in one lifetime.

Somehow while leaving the city of (precious few) angels we wound up off the interstate and on Highway 101. A station wagon pulled over and stopped in that precarious manner with too much of the car protruding into the road that is favored by many intoxicated Samaritans. We jumped in the back. Two men of Mexican descent were in the front. They were having a ball. Laughing. Yelling out the window and swaying the car side to side across the road for fun.

Turning around to face us the driver said, "Hey, you better put your seat belts on. We could be bumping into a few things. Ain't that right Gilbert? Oh Shit. This car don't have no seat belts. Oh well. Hey, where you going? San Francisco? Okay, let's go." And down went the pedal and off screeched the station wagon.

"We're going to stop at this store and get some beer. You want anything?" "Nope. We're all set." When our new friends returned they tossed a package of nylons to Theresa. "Here, I stole this for you." Then the driver slammed the car into reverse and crashed into a fence. "Ooops. You okay back there? Gotta wear your seat belt. No seatbelts in this car. Oh well. Wheeee!"

Before the advent of drunk driving laws, the roadways of this country between bar closing time and sunrise were the playgrounds of unbridled insanity. Have a tough week at work? Get hammered and get behind the wheel. What could go wrong? Glad you asked. The many variations of what could go wrong are documented in the police reports of every jurisdiction across this great land as well as in the hearts of the countless friends and family members who have lost someone to a drunk driver.

After some thoughts today on the obvious—how stupid it was back then and how much better it is now that everyone knows that there is a big price to pay for behaving that way—I thought about how few people who witnessed these episodes were sober enough to tell the tale. Gilbert and his friend wouldn't remember a thing. They would presumably wake up somewhere wondering where they were and how they got there with one of them asking the other, "did we pick up a couple of hippies last night?" And accident reports are by definition an after-the-fact activity. So the reporting on what happened in those hours in those days is left to the hitchhikers that no one remembers picking up who were frantically looking for a seat belt in the back of a freshly dented 1960s wood-paneled station wagon.

At sunrise we parted ways near San Jose. The night had bequeathed us her secrets for safe keeping with the understanding that we should wait a minimum of forty-five years before revealing them. The sun had chased away all of those colorful middle-of-the-night characters that might someday find a home in a Tom Waits song. Now she was illuminating the early to bed and early to rise folks whose stories are so infrequently considered songworthy.

Theresa was holding an egg-shaped container with her gifted nylons inside. We both began laughing. She said, "Now I'll have something to wear under my gown." She placed the egg at the base of a road sign. It was a thoughtful, albeit quizzical, gift for the next hitchhiker who came along and might, as one could easily imagine, be in need of new hosiery.

Then, a normal daytime person in a normal car who was not drunk pulled over and drove us to San Francisco within walking distance of the concert.

The concert was the stuff of legend. (Bob Dylan did show up.) By the end of it we had been awake for over thirty-five hours and had learned that the limit of our eighteen-year-old energy reserves was exactly 866 miles of straight hitchhiking followed by a day-long rock concert.

After a day of rest and a week of partying with our friends we headed back to Tucson (a trip that featured a much lengthier layover in Indio) and began making plans to hitchhike to Alaska because ... why the hell not?

When I say making plans what I mean is we looked on a map and saw that there was a road that went there.

Big Sur

We began this leg of our adventure in May. After a four-hour visit with some *new* friends on our favorite Indio on-ramp we were soon reunited with our *old* friends in San Francisco.

Eighteen years old, as free as free can be, hanging with our friends in America's coolest city … the partying was epic. So much so, and I know this is hard to believe, but after a week Theresa and I locked bloodshot eyes with each other and said, "We gotta get the hell away from here. How much Thunderbird wine can our metabolisms withstand?" (Side note and home improvement tip: The Thunderbird of this era cost two bucks a gallon. One night we spilled a full glass from the kitchen table. Within minutes the tiles on the floor started to buckle and come loose. I'm not sure if the classic wino Thunderbird is still available but if so, you might find that in addition to being an affordable aperitif, it is also an inexpensive and effective flooring adhesive remover.)

In the eight years between the *summer of love* and our arrival, San Francisco had experienced a significant exodus of peace and love. It was still a great place, especially the music scene, but the corner of Haight and Ashbury, while not exactly barbiturate-laden, was, shall we say, trending in that direction.

So off we went in the gradual and at times circuitous direction of Alaska. The plan was to begin by going places where walking down the street with your home on your back wouldn't cause the locals to drag their children indoors and call the authorities.

Embracing the era's tradition of nonconformity, we began our trip to America's most northern region by heading due south to Big Sur.

In 1975 it would have been damn near impossible to find a

larger concentration of people dedicating their lives to what would later be called new age pursuits than the cast of characters that had invaded this coastal California community.

The Esalen Institute was and still is located near some hot springs in Big Sur. It is a non-profit American retreat center and intentional community, which focuses on humanistic alternative education. What does that mean? No one knows. But what it meant to me at the time was that from there some deep-thinking naked hippies in hot springs were sending out cosmic vibes to every like-minded seeker on earth. If you were interested in personal growth, meditation, massage, yoga, psychology, ecology, spirituality, organic food, Eastern religions, alternative medicine and/or the exploration of human consciousness, you best be gassing up the Volkswagen van and following Esalen's beacon of positive energy (which is only visible to the truly enlightened) to this California epicenter of grooviness. (I believe that in the fine print of that cosmic beacon it says that in addition to your sleeping bag and your determination to enhance your personal evolution you should also bring your checkbook.)

The road had been patiently waiting for us to untether from the familiarity of what we had known so that it could begin to introduce us to people who were on a spiritual journey. In retrospect it would have been nice if our first introduction to this new world had been a bit more incremental. Our hasty transition from a world where it was normal to drink adhesive remover intentionally mislabeled as wine to an Esalen world so polar opposite was at best … unceremonious.

It seemed like the plan was to show us the end at the beginning and then see how close we could come to it via all the experiences the road intended to subject us to now that we were embracing it by relinquishing our San Francisco safety net.

We didn't know it, but we were taking our first steps on the well-worn route of personal discovery blazed by the countless flower children who came before us. That month we meandered up and down the coasts of California and Oregon which were saturated, infested, inundated, irretrievably overrun with what were in those days affectionately called freaks.

It seemed like every man who gave us a ride had long hair. Every woman wore Birkenstocks. Everyone used to live in Haight-Ashbury. Everyone had toured with The Grateful Dead. And everyone had a book to give us that "will change your life."

And we read them all—*Zen and the Art of Motorcycle Maintenance, Be Here Now, On the Road, The Dharma Bums*—all required reading for mid-seventies seekers. Each page of every book and all these encounters inching us away from what we had known and toward something we didn't know but thought might prove interesting.

During those traveling years our impressionable brains were forming an understanding of a world where yes was the answer to the question, adventure was its own reward, trusting that things would work out was the only way to view a situation, and almost everyone was a potential good Samaritan.

I estimate that during that first year we travelled between fifteen and twenty thousand miles entirely on the wings of kindness.

The Seventies

That last line about the wings of kindness reminded me of a reoccurring post-hitchhiking encounter.

On the rare occasions when Theresa and I are telling road stories, my sister-in-law will encourage us to stop romanticizing those years and ask, for the sake of our impressionable nieces and nephews, that we at least include some details about how difficult and scary it was. "Tell them that it wasn't all 'awesome' please."

She's right. The forty-five years that have passed since then have engendered a tendency in us to deemphasize the difficulties and overglorify the fun stuff. So for the sake of all the parents who would prefer that their children experience worldly adventures in ways that induce fewer sleepless nights for their loved ones, here is a chapter that focuses on a couple of notable negative experiences.

During these three years we were pounded by the elements, unable to keep more than a tent wall between us and marauding bears, and we were at the mercy of everyone we encountered. Later you'll learn how we had deadly chemicals crop-dusted on us, and that we contracted amoebic dysentery and wasted away for six weeks. All of this could have been avoided without losing any of the adventure if we weren't hitchhiking. Young people all over the world are taking advantage of technology via ride sharing and other apps to travel in a manner that minimizes their exposure to unnecessary risk without diminishing their experience. As an added benefit, their parents sleep a little easier. Today you can travel the world … and still be nice to your mom.

I've chosen two incidents to establish my theory that it is much better to be a young adult today than it was in the sixties and seventies—especially in the realm of personal freedom.

In the sixties and seventies, you could get ten years for two joints. (Now weed is legal or decriminalized in much of the country.)

You had no legal right to marry your same-sex soul mate. (Now same-sex marriage is legal in all fifty states.)

There was a draft.

The same year (1967) that the *summer of love* was happening in San Francisco the state of Virginia was at the Supreme Court vociferously defending its law banning interracial marriage.

The list of oppressive laws and fear-based societal norms that are relegated to history now but had to be dodged and endured and protested and fought against in court back then far outnumber the things that are disproportionately glorified from that era.

It must be said that we all owe a debt of gratitude to the members of the movements of the sixties for initiating the battles that eventually brought these changes to the world. But, again, in my opinion, it is better to be a young adult in the era that benefitted from the decades of work that was begun in the sixties and seventies than it was to be a young adult in the tumultuous, transitional era that initiated the battles.

I had long hair. Can anyone under the age of thirty comprehend that this would be a problem? Let us journey to the panhandle of Texas in 1975 for a retrospective tutorial. We got a ride from a local Texan. He brought us to a diner and bought us lunch. The guy behind the counter hated us. You could actually see it. It looked like waves of heat rising from his head and shoulders. If we weren't being chaperoned by a verifiably bonafide good ole boy the least that would have happened is that he would have refused to serve us, the worst …

After being served some greasy food cooked with hatred and tossed in front of us with palpable disdain, I asked, as politely and respectfully as possible, if I could use the rest room. The unspoken part of his response was "It's bad enough I had to serve

you and your hussy but the rest room is not for dirty hippies."
The spoken part was an emphatic "No! And if you go out back
to piss I got a big dog back there who'll tear you to bits."

Think about the weight of the chill that followed on the
mind of a kid thousands of miles from home. It took seven
footsteps to get from the counter to the door. Each one of those
slow-motion, fear-filled steps drove a little deeper into my heart
a permanent change that altered me in ways I recognize but can't
explain.

Now let's visit rural Arizona, shall we? There are truck stops
in the middle of the desert there with parking lots so vast they
can accommodate hundreds of eighteen-wheelers. These great
big diesel-smelling neon islands are designed to fulfill the needs
of cross-country haulers. They feature such amenities as showers,
rooms you can rent by the hour, a diner with a conspicuous
absence of vegetarian fare, and very friendly women in short
dresses who do not seem to suffer from a fear of strangers.

We were dropped off at one of these iconic bastions of
Americana just before sunset. We decided to get a cup of coffee
and a muffin before moving on. As we walked up to the diner
we could see that it was bustling. We set our backpacks against
the outside of the building near a big window so we could keep
an eye on them from inside. When we opened the door and
entered, forty conversations abruptly ceased. Every pair of eyes
followed us as we found a booth and sat down.

I remember thinking how fortunate I had been to have lived
eighteen years before finally experiencing the hatred of a room
full of people who had never seen me before—a hatred so intense
that my presence in their neon paradise made it impossible for
any of them to continue to eat their big hunks of gravy-sopped
meat.

No one talked. No one ate. And no one came to serve us. At

first we thought that perhaps we had to order at the counter but after other patrons came in and were served at their tables the true nature of our situation became clear.

We had left peace-y, love-y northern California, and were now all alone in mean-spirited mid-nineteen-seventies America—a club where hating people who looked like us earned you a lifetime membership and all the benefits and goodwill that came with it.

The saving grace of our Texas diner episode was that we weren't alone. But the degree of all-alone-in-the-world that we experienced in that Arizona truck stop, at that moment, with those Americans, was soul-crushing.

As we watched more people enter and be served by the waitress, we faced a choice. We could ask to be served under the ridiculous assumption that it had been an honest mistake and they just didn't notice us (a decision that would surely increase the odds of a confrontation) or we could make that long lonesome walk across the floor. There was really no choice. We got up and with every eye fixed upon us we departed, handing another small victory to mob rule and the power of mean-spirited ignorance. As gravied meat returned to mouths of what were once our fellow patrons, we lifted our packs upon our backs and walked past dozens of idling semitrucks to the crossroads where we stood under a road sign that had three bullet holes in it.

That was forty-five years ago. I still have long hair. I have sat in diners with it graying on top of my head in Alabama, Kentucky, Tennessee, Georgia, and Texas. I have ordered food in these places using my unapologetic Boston accent and not once was I treated with anything but courtesy and civility. America may become worse than it was back then but right now, despite the challenges that are before us, these days are better.

Beth and Patrick

In those early days the west coast from Santa Cruz to Vancouver was North America's comfort zone for us. The places where we felt safe in the rest of the country were concentrated in and near college towns. Among these academic strongholds of non-coastal Ram Dass-iness, none was spoken about with more reverence at the time than Boulder, Colorado. So it was only natural that we would include a stop there on our way to Alaska. We had every intention of drinking deeply of Boulder's storied esoteric offerings …

But. The. Rain.

It welcomed us to Colorado by pummeling us as soon as we crossed the border from New Mexico. For the next three days it exploited our inability to find shelter and asserted its authority over us with an unrelenting and callous disregard for our well-being. We stood in the rain. We set our tent up in the rain. We spit toothpaste out of our mouths onto the ground in the morning in the rain. We ate moist granola and soggy peanut butter sandwiches under bridges in the freaking rain.

"I know that Boulder is a place that we should experience but the hell with this. We can swing through here on our way back from Alaska. That'll be two months from now. It may have stopped raining by then." "Okay let's get out of here. There's a diner. Let's get a cup of coffee and dry off a bit first."

We leaned our backpacks against the inside wall by the door where they dripped a river of water onto the floor. We sat at the counter in our wet raincoats while the storm beat against the door threatening us by name. The waitress was a thin blonde woman. She brought us coffee and went into the kitchen while we wrapped our hands around the hot cups hoping that the heat might find its way into our damp bones. Ten minutes later she returned with two plates brimming with scrambled eggs, bacon, home fries and toast. We hadn't ordered breakfast. We had no money for that sort of luxury. She slid the plates gently and lovingly in front of us and smiled as she watched our faces through the rising steam.

Remembering this moment so soon after writing about that Texas diner experience has made me a bit weepy.

I said that the Texas diner episode altered me in ways I recognize but can't explain. Now, by way of *A Tale of Two Diners*, I think I can. That guy served us our food the way a prison guard would to a convicted murderer in the 1700s. It was like he opened the slot at the bottom of the cell door and slid it across the floor. We couldn't eat it. It was poisoned with hatred. If I hadn't watch him cook it, I would have been afraid that he spit in it. He treated us like rodents and made it clear that if given the chance he would show us the same level of humanity he would to a rat in his cupboard.

But the food we were served from this angel of a waitress in Boulder was so enriched with love and human kindness that we felt it could have sustained us for a week. The moment by itself was simply a kind gesture from a stranger but now when placed beside the other it created a stark contrast and a testimony to the power of love over hate. More importantly, it was a reminder to us that we were deserving of kindness. The place in my heart that carried the emotional emptiness of being treated as worse than worthless had just been nourished by human decency and scrambled eggs. It was the most delicious food I ever ate.

Say what you want about hippies. (They do make it easy to make fun of them.) But if you live in a part of this country where you are despised by the community because you're not like everyone else, you probably won't know the true extent of the damage that living beneath the weight of that hatred does to your psyche until you move to a town full of easy-to-mock hippies and experience the kind of generosity, kindness, and human decency that you (and everyone) deserve.

The waitress's name was Beth. We told her that we had decided to head north until we found the sun because Colorado weather seemed to have a personal vendetta against us, and we had been waterlogged for so long that we couldn't take it anymore. A few minutes later she handed me a piece of paper and said, "These are directions to my house. The door is unlocked. Go there and dry off. My husband will be home before me. His name is Patrick. I'll see you tonight."

We followed the directions, walking through driving sheets of malevolent rain. We entered the house, put on dry clothes, sat in real chairs, boiled water from a real faucet in a real teapot on a real stove and told each other that if this was a dream we should try not to wake up for a while.

Patrick came home and treated us as if we were friends he had known all his life.

As hard as they tried, my defense mechanisms couldn't convince me that I shouldn't trust these folks. I kept saying to my skeptical survival skills, in response to their pleas for caution, that not only couldn't they sniff out any reason to doubt that Beth and Patrick were anything but what they seemed—a completely open, honest, trusting, and trustworthy young couple—but ... Theresa, whom we both agreed was the last word on who to feel safe around, adored them. Even my fine-tuned, highly experienced, inner security detail, with their deeply engrained cynicism, were loath to challenge the judgment of the girl who grew up in the projects and whose instincts were damn near infallible in this arena.

We felt so at home with them. One of the most important skills necessary to survive the life we were living was to decipher as quickly as possible how much of who we really were was safe or advantageous to reveal in each situation. Within the home of these folks, we were able to let our guard down and be ourselves. It was my first real extended taste of that Woodstock Nation, love-can-build-a-better-world thing that I hoped against hope I would find beyond the world I had known.

We were approximately one month into what would turn out to be three years of road living. Our stay in Boulder was the time when extraordinary people started intersecting with, and dramatically influencing, our lives so frequently that we would soon come to expect it.

*****

Our procuring of shelter took all the fun out of drenching the streets of Boulder and persuaded the storm to head east toward Kansas in search of new transients to bully.

We stayed with those two angels for three days. When we were thawed out, nourished, rested, still young and itching to move, we ventured out to find an abandoned mining camp, hidden high in the Rocky Mountains, recommended to us by our new best friends.

This was the beginning of a pattern that would reoccur for the next three years. Interesting people would take us in and then, after some subtle assessing of our worthiness, would grant us access to their favorite secret paradise. We were frequently being handed the equivalent of treasure maps, scribbled on the back of envelopes, guiding us to places that would never be included in a tourist brochure.

A lot of the folks who opened the doors of their worlds to us had previously lived the road life but were now putting down roots because of job or family responsibilities. We saw them as the elders of our tribe. Our stories of current-day life on the road would ignite their memories and often expose a visible longing in their eyes. The sharing of off-the-beaten-trail hiding places was the kind of insider gifting they had been the recipients of when the highway was their home. It was as if they had been waiting for us to appear so they could pay it forward. Looking back at them from an on-ramp while their children waved and called our names out of the windows of their family car was always a tender moment. The same road that would bring them back to the life they were building for their families was about to carry us to an adventure they had made possible but could not share. Circumstances would limit their participation to the confines of vicariousness.

So, how cool was the place Beth and Patrick sent us? Oh man!

We hitchhiked until the mountain road became too narrow to accommodate automobiles. Then we started walking … up. The highest elevation in New England is Mount Washington at just over six thousand feet. Boulder, Colorado, our starting point, sits at five thousand three hundred feet. Our destination was at ten thousand feet. So there was a whole lot of *up* to be trod.

When we set up camp the first night, at around eight thousand feet, it started to snow. (It's the elevation stupid.) Inside of our screen-covered tent, with unshared thoughts of hypothermia, we had just pressed our skinny bodies together in a shivering embrace when we heard something—not a bear, not a hungry mountain lion, not the ghost of a long-dead prospector— a dog. A small, black, friendly, snow-covered dog. We let him in where he stayed until morning, providing us one-third of the warmth necessary for what was, in our opinion, more of a three-dog night.

In the morning our canine friend, displaying the kind of common sense that consistently eluded people like us, respectfully declined to ascend the mountain, and trotted downward in the direction of warmer temperatures.

We reached the abandoned mining camp just before sunset. There was a small cabin there where hikers and fugitives could find shelter. Inside we found some thoughtful gifts left with love by previous dwellers. The two Lipton tea bags hanging from the wall on a nail silently proclaimed that they had only been used for one cup of tea and that you, dear fugitives, were welcome to boil the remaining flavor out for one final weak but soothing cup.

That night an incandescent full moon slowly rose over the majestic peaks and lit our new home as if it were midday. The view, the moonlight, the moment in time were ... how do you say something is greater than spectacular? The view, the moonlight, the moment in time were *spectacular times ten*. It wasn't just what we were seeing and how it made us feel. It was that no one else was there. This was our own private moonlit mountain. The love of strangers had pulled us in and gifted the place *and* the moment to us.

And then ... because the universe couldn't stop showing how much it loved us, we noticed that a shadow was beginning to move across the moon.

Over the course of six days, we had been plucked from the torrential elements, given all the comforts of home, guided to a magical location in the mountains, and were about to be given a command performance by the solar system. That's right, on the night that we were five thousand feet closer to the stars than we had ever been, we found ourselves wide-eyeing each other with mouths agape during our moment of mutual realization. We were experiencing a full lunar eclipse.

Sitting on a rock beside the cabin with our arms around each other in our spectacular-times-ten Rocky Mountain paradise while watching a surprise lunar eclipse was a powerful indication that, if given a chance, the road would deliver experiences to us that would reinforce the idea that miracles are everywhere and each one has something to teach us about who we are, who we have been, and who we could be.

We witnessed the shadow of the earth block the brightest full moon we had ever seen while we were four thousand feet higher than the summit of Mount Washington. It felt as if the galaxy had dropped the curtain down on the story of the life we had known. When the shadow had passed and the moon relit the mountain, we felt that we had just been shown a glimpse into the possibilities that awaited us on our improbable journey, and ... that the working-class kids from a factory town, who saw the world through the tainted lenses of what their childhoods had taught them, had just been relegated to a who-we-used-to-be archive. The door was now open to the unlimited possibilities of who we could become.

After descending back to Boulder, we stayed with Beth and Patrick a few more days before heading north. We would visit with them again later that year. That second time they said, "We're going to hitchhike back to Wisconsin to see our families. Give us a ride to the highway in our car and stay here in our house for as long as you want." We dropped them off on the ramp to the interstate. We never saw them again.

If Beth and Patrick are still alive and are reading this, here's a great big SMOOCH for you both from a couple of grandparents who remember you with much, much love.

Montana

Prior to our departure from Beth and Patrick's unconditional love sanctuary we had been traveling between relatively safe bastions of what would now be called progressive thought. After we left Boulder, we did not encounter anything resembling a college town for three months. We spent all of June discovering the America that existed in the mountain west. What we learned from the data accrued from those weeks in Wyoming, Idaho, Colorado, Nevada, and Montana shaped the entire future of our hitchhiking experience.

In that part of the country, although we had the same amount of nothing in common that we had with Texans and Arizonans, we didn't experience any direct hatred. (To be fair, aside from the characters in the two diner stories, we met lots of sweet, kind, and generous people in both of those states.) In the mountain west we grew accustomed to receiving just as much kindness and generosity from people with whom we had nothing in common as we had been shown by our fellow West Coast freaks. And not a single one of these rural mountain Americans gave us a book to read that would "change our lives." It was a refreshing and endearing difference.

If the goal was to expand our understanding of the world, wasn't destinationing from college town to college town playing it safe and limiting our growth potential? Theresa and I agreed that yes was the answer to that question. And so we began to seek out and embrace the unfamiliar. This decision was made easier by early June. By then we had come to realize that, as easy as it was for some folks to be disgusted or outraged by their interpretations of who we were and what evil or downfall of societal norms we represented, there were lots of other folks who thought we were adorable. I'm sure that many people who would never consider picking up a hitchhiker had to fight off a strong urge to stop and pinch us both on the cheek. We were usually smiling and laughing. Sometimes Theresa would be twirling in a summer dress to a song she was humming. We made eye contact with you in a way that indicated that not only were we not psycho murderers but that we were having the time of our life, that the sun loved us, and for the small price of a ride down the road we would inject beams of infectious joy and the love of living into your life which, not to be judgmental, probably was a bit wanting in that department. To a certain, larger-than-you-would-think section of the driving public we were pretty darn irresistible.

In the fifteen seconds motorists had to decide whether or not to open the doors of their world to us, what they saw was partly a true reflection of who we were and partly a calculated exaggeration of it. This was a job—the primary requirement of which was to appear safe to strangers. The secondary, but more effective when refined, was to create an image that would tap into a person's curiosity and create the thought that later, in the quiet of their presumably less exciting lives, they would regret having passed us by.

When a car would pull over, I would go to the passenger window and in the most disarming and friendly manner I would ask how far the person was going. Job one was to alleviate their apprehension as quickly as possible. I became an expert at this. There was more to it than smiling and being friendly. It was an attitude—I intentionally projected a combination of being perfectly happy to stay where I was but excited about the possibility of meeting someone new if that was what happened. There could never be even the slightest hint of desperation or suspicion. And certainly nothing that might be misinterpreted as nefarious. It's an art that the road taught me that I have used whenever applicable throughout my entire adult life.

It hardly ever mattered how far the person was going. We would take rides that were only headed down the road a quarter mile just for a change of scenery. I asked the question in case I saw or sensed something that triggered my suspicions about the car or the driver or the other passengers. If so, I would stay in character but say, "Thanks so much, but we're going to wait till we get a ride to ..." (someplace further than they were going).

Some of the things that would increase the odds of the ride being a less-than-perfect experience were obvious—more than one adult male in the car, or open whiskey bottles. But in most cases I had to trust my instinct. I grew up in a place where strong people would punch weak people just for fun. I was a small kid. I always trusted my instinct to give me advance warning for when it was time to go. So picking up on bad vibes isn't a vague hippie term to me. It's the reason I have lived long enough to tell this story.

Some cars had two or three long-haired dudes in them and I would accept the ride because I knew they were of the Beth and Patrick tribe and it was going to be great.

Other times when the same number of long-haired dudes were in a car, we wouldn't get in. Remember, I came from a place where many long-hairs were addicted to barbiturates. I knew the difference.

Theresa and I both had rings that when turned over could pass for wedding bands. I always introduced her as my wife. For a lot of people we were the first hitchhikers they ever spoke to. In 1975 the one thing about hippies that probably stuck in the mind of a middle-aged guy coming home from a bar after work was that they were into free love. We always presumed that asking a hippie's girlfriend for some of "that there free love" would be easier than asking a hippie's wife.

I would load in our backpacks and sit beside the driver. Theresa only entered after everything else was inside. If there were no passengers and the driver was a man, I would always sit beside him. If it was a truck or a car with a bench seat, Theresa would sit to my right so he would have to reach over me to touch her. No one ever did that.

In almost every state and province that we passed through at least one person offered to let us stay at their home. I was, especially in this first year, always inclined to say yes. It happened so often and was almost always a good experience that I may have been guilty of some complacency. Every now and then, after a driver had offered us lodging, and before I had responded, I would feel a pinch or an elbow pressing into my side and would know that Theresa's acute, street-smart survival instinct had picked up on something from this person that I was not seeing. I would then politely decline the offer because I was just smart enough to know that she was smarter.

My Boston Accent

Many people who picked us up out west had a chip on their shoulder about people from back east and more specifically New Yorkers. I suspected that if some of these folks were asked to draw a map of the northeast everything from Maryland to Maine would be one big scowling New York City.

Confrontation is no friend to a person thousands of miles from home. I didn't need to be taught how to avoid it. I'd been doing that as a survival skill since grade school. But now I had to up my game because the confrontations I was experienced in avoiding to this point didn't suffer under the unendurable delusion that New York City was the source of evil in the world or that I was from there.

That made my Boston accent, which I had always worn as a badge of honor, a tremendous liability. But since Massachusetts and New York City were apparently the same place, and because of that I would be subjected on a regular basis to variations of the tale of the rich guy from New York who bought up the land that "I been hunting on since I was a kid and then told me I couldn't hunt there no more … and then he came to the town meeting and wanted us to put a stop light in the middle of Main Street."

I know these are real issues and I'm not minimizing the detrimental effect that outside money can have on a rural community. But come on. I have six bucks in my pocket. The only thing I have in common with rich New Yorkers is that *you* can't tell the difference in our accents.

My regional mutilation of the king's English was subjecting me to a potentially dangerous level of stupid. My first thought was that it had to go. But I started thinking about how much I love the fact that I don't sound like everyone else. And then, in defiance of the forces that were trying to convince me that my accent had no redeeming or useful qualities, I decided that the best course of action was to learn how to turn it on and off as needed.

I vowed to become bilingual.

Night after night I tried to get the muscles in my mouth to contort into the unnatural shape that would allow me to pronounce that pesky letter R. I repeated these words over and over (not ovah and ovah): Water, not Waddah. Quarter, not Quaddah. And the most difficult word in the English language for a Bostonian to pronounce, warbler, not wawhblah.

Eventually I developed a fragile but promising relationship with R. And together we depalooka'd my verbiage to the point where I became fluent in Bostonian *and* English. With the support and assistance of my new favorite letter, I was now able to avoid becoming a receptacle for the universal contempt that some westerners have for that million-mile imaginary Gomorrah back east.

From this point forward I concealed my accent. There was never a good reason to speak in my native tongue. It would have been easy to lose it completely. But I hung on to it because I knew that in my subsequent life it would be a valuable asset when used strategically.

When I know that the person I'm doing business with equates my accent with a lack of sophistication, I turn it loose. There is nothing more advantageous in business than being underestimated. This is a tool I've seen used masterfully by some brilliant southerners who exaggerate their drawl to reinforce an unobservant yankee's inaccurate preconception of their capabilities and thereby gain the upper hand.

*****

With my modified accent in place and our new hunger for things and places we'd never seen before, we continued heading north toward Alaska. But first—a memorable stopover in Montana.

Every state seemed to have its own horror story about hitchhikers that drivers felt compelled to share with us. Montana had the best. It was the story of a guy who picked up two hitchhikers—"a man and a woman just like you"—who killed the driver and ate his heart.

My primary responsibility as a passenger was to make the driver feel safe. My ability to do so was made significantly more difficult when his first words implied that my girlfriend and I might be plotting to forcibly remove and fricassee his giblets.

I wanted to say, "relax, we're vegetarians." But I didn't for two reasons. One, I had a very short leash on my wise-ass mouth at the time, having learned the hard way that what I think is funny was often not given the appreciation it deserved by the general public, and could often cause a situation to become awkward. Two, it was rural Montana in the mid-seventies. Even though the internal organs of the residents of big sky country were obviously and verifiably not vegetables, I feared that most folks we met would probably lump vegetarians into the same category as voracious, organ-harvesting hitchhikers since they had likely never met a person who was skilled in either vocation.

In 1975 Ringling, Montana had forty residents. According to last year's census it now has thirty-five. While many parts of America have seen migratory influxes that the locals would claim have changed the character of the town for the worse, not so with Ringling.

After our driver had finished telling us Montana's prize-winning hitchhiker horror story, he dropped us off in Ringling. Jimmy Buffett had written a song about the town. That was enough for us to decide to go into its only bar to have a beer and check it out. It was there that we met Ms. Ginny Rhinegold.

Every mile northward that we travelled on the continent exposed us to less weed and more alcohol. Envelope please. The winner in the category of state or province with the highest and most unrepentant, reckless over-consumption of booze witnessed by Don and Theresa on their North American travels, goes to … Newfoundland! Coming in a close second and worthy of honorable mention is the great state of Montana.

It was mid-afternoon. Aside from us, there was a bartender and a woman who looked to be in her late sixties sitting at the end of the bar on a stool that may have had her name on it. We ordered beers and enjoyed pleasant conversation with the barman. (After ensuring him that we had no interest in his internal organs.) Ginny joined the conversation and took a liking to us right away. She offered us a place to stay and some money if I would help her shovel out some mud from her basement. We agreed and after another beer, which she was kind enough to buy us, and after listening to Jimmy Buffett's tribute to the hometown of Ms. Rhinegold on the jukebox, we entered the world of a woman who was born in and had never left a town of forty people.

I shoveled mud from her basement for a few hours. We spent the night with her. She drank cans of Olympia beer the entire time. (Including the one she poured into a glass at 7:00 the next morning, enriching it with her daily allotment of protein by cracking a raw egg over it before chugging the whole thing down in one long gulp. Ahhh, the breakfast of champions.)

I felt just as comfortable with Ms. Rhinegold as I did with Beth and Patrick but for wildly different reasons. I knew instinctively that I could be myself around my Colorado hippie friends even though I had had no previous exposure to people like them. Ginny Rhinegold was a big-hearted, working-class alcoholic. There was no segment of society with which I was more familiar. I felt like a cusp species. What I came from and what I was becoming were equally capable of providing me with a sense of home via entirely disparate environments.

*****

Empowered with twenty whole dollars, we caught a ride down the road to White Sulphur Springs from a man and a woman in their late twenties who suggested, you guessed it, that we stop in one of the town's four bars and get hammered.

I got drunk for the first time when I was fourteen. I quit drinking when I was thirty-three. Contained within those nine-teen years is a ton of stupid and a mountain of selfish. Especially selfish. Getting drunk is all about being selfish.

It would be nice if the trajectory of a man's journey to becoming a person he can be proud of was a straight line that went directly from the person he didn't want to be to the one he hoped he could be. Unfortunately, my route looks more like the graph of a twenty-year financial investment portfolio—the trend over decades is gradually upward with dramatic plummets along the way.

We went to the bar. We drank till midnight. All four of us stumbled a few houses down from the bar to crash at the house of the couple. After twenty minutes … (because … stupid/ selfish/inconsiderate) I decided to go back to the bar and drink till closing time. At two in the morning I staggered back to the house and fell into bed. The next day I learned that the woman whose house we were in was married to a different guy from the town and, because her boyfriend hadn't heard me leave, when I came back he thought I might be the husband and had his pistol cocked and aimed at the bedroom door.

So, there you go. Drunk plus stupid plus selfish plus a lack of consideration for others equals being one index finger movement away from getting a bullet in the head.

The Free Camp

Checklist of threatening things a person might encounter on a three-year North American hitchhiking adventure.

If you have had previous experience with any of the following, check the corresponding box.

Ignorance – Check.

Alcoholics – Check. Check.

Men trying to get rid of you and keep your girl – Check. Check. Check.

Bears – Wait. What?

Bears. Well, I've dealt with people who had similar intellectual capacities and with people who would snatch a sandwich out of your hand and dare you to do something about it because they were bigger than you and feral. But actual giant, fur-covered, cave-dwelling, hibernating, long-clawed, sharp-toothed bears? Nope. Never had the pleasure.

That's a shame because when you get to the Canadian Rockies, you're going to meet a lot of them and the diplomacy skills you have relied so heavily upon to navigate danger will be entirely ineffective. Because bears have a voracious appetite for everything except well-reasoned arguments as to why their brutish behavior is hurtful to fellow mammals.

*****

How do you address the challenge of keeping vagabonds separated from tourists in your national park or forest?

In the United States, you encourage law enforcement to enforce the kind of laws that are written to target the segment of the population that in previous generations were called vagrants.

In mature, reasonable, Canada, you designate a couple of acres of woods, a safe distance away from the fully equipped tourist campgrounds, where people of little or no means can camp for free.

Between 1973 and 1982 the Canadian government provided a free alternate campground at all their big outdoorsy tourist destinations.

We hiked into the Jasper, Alberta Free Camp in late June. There were outhouses and a spigot for water and, to the best of my recollection, nothing else.

We walked through this sprawling collection of campsites that featured a colorful variety of improvised shelters cobbled together with tarps and twine and all manner of itinerant ingenuity. It was like a government-sanctioned hobo jungle without the hobos. We had seen real hobo encampments in freight yards before. The people we met in them were often intense with a sense of desperation hanging over them. We never lingered. But this place had a great feel to it. It was an eclectic assemblage of hikers, woodsmen, and seekers. Being it was Canada in 1975, one would think there may have been a few draft dodgers on the grounds as well.

While we were searching out a spot to set up our tent, we were commenting on how almost all the campsites had lovely glass bottles of different colors and shapes dangling in little bunches on their peripheries. It seemed artsy to us.

A couple of hours after we had set up our tiny tent, two men in their late twenties from Michigan arrived and set up next to us. I was writing deep thoughts in a journal. Theresa was sitting on a tree stump reading a book. Our campsite had a dreamy butterfly kind of feel to it.

They assembled their camp with a focus and a sense of urgency that was more worker bee than butterfly. As soon as their tent was raised and secured, one of them emerged from it with a hatchet in hand and proceeded to chop down a tree about twenty feet high and six inches in diameter. He trimmed off all the branches until it was a long pole. And then, through some wizardry that included the use of ropes, slip knots, and the scaling of giant trees, the two of them hung a perfectly level twenty-foot homemade pole fifteen feet off the ground between two giant fir trees.

"You folks have a bear pole set up for your food and backpacks?"

"Huh? A bear what?"

"Bear pole like this." He pointed.

Me and my flower child looked at each other and shook our heads.

"No. We don't have one of those."

"Grab your stuff and bring it here and we'll hang it for you."

Again, as if they were living in a time-lapsed video, they used rope magic to hang all four of our back-packs at the center point of the pole because, we later learned, since the center can't be reached from either tree, our supplies would be subject to pillaging only by the type of bears who had a background in tightrope walking or pole dancing. (The horizontal kind. Not the kind you're thinking of.)

As fond as we were of the free camp, our fondness paled in comparison to the affection felt by the community of bears who lived in the area. To us it was a free camp. To them it was a free buffet. They saw it as an open-air market of deliciousness. They would go to the big shiny motor home campground during the day and pose for photos in return for peanut butter sandwiches made for them by tourists. Then unruly gangs of them would come marauding through the free camp at night to pillage and plunder and lay waste to our tarpaulin village.

I had never thought about the term *babes in the wood* before. But that's what we were. Sensing our obvious lack of wilderness training, and not wanting to witness a mauling, our Michigan mountain men took us under their proverbial wings. Without their protection and tutelage, Jasper's marauding bear gangs would certainly have had their way with us.

That evening our neighbors gave us a crash course on how to protect our food and our bodies from the local behemoths who were determined to make the gentrifying of their neighborhood as costly as possible.

"Wear a bell on your backpack when hiking so you don't surprise them."

"Always hang your food."

"And remember that the stories about bears smelling and attacking menstruating women have never been proven to be true."

"Okay. Good. Thanks."

The next evening just after sunset we heard yelling and what sounded like pots clanging from the far end of the campground. Then we heard someone scream, "BEAR DOG!" What immediately followed was the sound of a dog barking and an exponential increase in the amount and the volume of yelling and clanging.

The glass bottles that hung in bunches on the periphery of the homes of experienced free campers, although quite artsy, were actually an early warning system to alert the camper to the presence of tiptoeing bears. He or she would hear the bottles clink, spy the intruder, and set off a chain reaction throughout the camp by banging two metal pans together while yelling threats and obscenities at the bear and calling for the bear dog.

What's a bear dog? Good question. This particular evening it was an Irish setter who lived for the thrill of chasing a bear through, and eventually out of, the camp.

A bear tripped the glass bottle alarm system and was immediately set upon by a screaming, pot-clanging draft dodger and an Irish setter. It was a call to arms. Beginning with the campers closest to the initial incident, residents began yelling and clanging pots to encourage the bear to find an escape route that didn't go through their campsite. "Don't chase him over here! Clang! Clang! Curse word! Curse word!" In seconds, three hundred campers, in fear of having their flimsy living quarters trampled by a nine-hundred-pound rampaging leviathan, had turned the entire site into an obscenity-yelling, pot-clanging, barking cacophony.

As we (you know, the babes in the wood) stood dumbstruck, having no idea what was happening, we saw a mammoth brown bear running at full speed directly toward our campsite while swiping his long claws behind him at a red dog who was having the greatest moment of his life. We stepped aside and both pursuer and pursued ran past us close enough that, had we thought of it, we could have patted both of their heads. A few minutes later the clanging and yelling tapered off and ceased. Everyone went back to cooking dinner. Then the bear dog swaggered back with a bounce in his step and a chest full of pride. He stopped at every campsite to garner head pats and words of praise from grateful residents. "Good boy. That's a good bear dog."

We didn't know what had just happened or what kind of surrealistic film we had been unwittingly cast in. But we knew that we had just experienced something that had been entirely beyond our ability to predict and that we were a *long* way from home.

*****

These days, a few clicks on a keyboard can move money around the world in an instant. In the nineteen seventies, except for Western Union, money meandered, it dawdled, it took time to smell the roses. Money was mellow back then dude.

As we ran low, we would spend the last of our mellow money on beans, rice, peanut butter, granola, and lentils. With a good supply of nonperishables, and without a penny, we settled into the Free Camp while the money order my mother mailed to us in care of General Delivery, Jasper, Alberta, casually took in the sights en route to our mountain enclave.

Many of the fellow travelers we had met in the lower forty-eight were variations of your Esalen types—sweet seekers who were primarily cerebral. There were a lot of deep thoughts crackling back there behind their tie-dyed headbands. I suspect that all that thinking had brought many of them to the realization that, without the benefit of a reliable motor vehicle and financial resources, the wilderness at the upper reaches of the planet could and would knock an enlightened spiritual wanderer down a few notches from the top of the food chain and thereby increase the possibility of a hastened farewell to one's mortal coil.

Their informed circumspection regarding the northern reaches of the continent, with her unforgiving thousand-mile expanses between supplies, and her leveling of the playing field between man and beast, seemed to filter out a lot of them. The further north we journeyed the fewer of these folks we encountered.

From Jasper north the travelers we encountered all had the same hunger for learning about and experiencing the world beyond their hometowns, but they seemed to have a stronger connection to the part of their blood that hadn't repressed or forgotten the pioneers in their lineage.

Until now, our youthfulness had created and sustained a blind eye to mortality. We felt invincible. Sporting a cavalier disdain for due diligence, we would throw ourselves into new situations with no preparation and learn as we went. At best it was a way to accelerate our growth. At worst … well, you know.

The bears of the Canadian Rockies did for us what no amount of hateful diner owners or bully rain or mountain snow or stories about murdered hitchhikers could have done. They made us realize that Mother Nature has a long history of applying the principles of natural selection to ensure the survival of the species by killing off the unprepared before they can reproduce offspring too stupid to survive.

When we walked out of the Free Camp to hitchhike to Alaska, we left behind our youthful delusions of immortality and our dangerously misinformed preconceptions of where we stood in the hierarchy of living things.

The Alaska-Canada Highway

I have seen, driven on, stood beside, bounced untethered in the back of pickup trucks for miles upon, and inhaled deep into my lungs the dust of, many dirt roads in my life. But never could I have imagined a stretch of gravel as impressive as the Alaska-Canada Highway.

When we set out to hitchhike this beast in 1975 it was approximately fourteen hundred miles of dirt. If a similar road extended west from Boston, your tires would not touch asphalt till you reached Omaha.

Of course, it's all paved now. Which means that North America is no longer able to provide a similar experience to the one Theresa and I had in July of that year.

Not only was it unpaved but, being the only land route for supplies destined for Alaska, it attracted a very special breed of unhinged truck drivers who drove it at high speeds with an attitude that was just a smidgen beneath reckless abandon. The first time we were nearly blown off the side of the road and into the Yukon wilderness by a truck driving seventy miles per hour, pulling three fully loaded trailers, on this epic stretch of gravel, we knew we were entering a world peopled with a tribe of humans we had not previously encountered.

A second impossible-to-ignore indication that our docket of new experiences would soon include a series of fresh entries were the road signs. The first one we leaned our backpacks against had taken at least one and possibly two shotgun blasts, permanently relinquishing its intended information to the realm of conjecture.

Standing beneath a bullet-riddled sign that drunks, kids, moms, and clergymen shot at out the passenger window with a nonchalance reminiscent of the way most folks would wave to a neighbor was a bit intimidating and spoke volumes.

The sun never set while we were in Northern British Columbia, Yukon, and Alaska. It exposed the vastness of the land in dramatic fashion. We would crest a mountain and see before us an expanse of wilderness extending to another mountain range on the horizon. It would take twelve hours of driving to crest that mountain where the midnight sun would reveal another impossible stretch of wilderness between us and another mountain range twelve hours of driving away.

There is a sulphur hot spring alongside the AlCan highway in Northern British Columbia called Liard. Today there are changing stations, wheelchair access, a campground, a play-ground, and a restaurant. To my recollection, when our driver pulled over and said he wanted us to experience something spe-cial, there was a wooden boardwalk to the site (built for walking over wet ground by the army in 1942) and not much else.

We walked a short distance through swamp and boreal forest. You could feel the heat before the path opened to reveal a pool of water with steam rising from it. A stream fed the area so you could get warmer or cooler by swimming toward or away from the hot spring. Sulphur, in case you don't know, smells like rotten eggs. In my life I have had more than my share of rotten egg experiences. This would turn out to be my favorite.

Theresa had told me that when she was a little girl she loved the TV westerns and stories about pioneers in wagon trains. Before she was old enough to know that she had been born a century too late she was sure that when she grew up she would be a pioneer woman.

Here we were—two kids from Lynn, Massachusetts, holding our bodies against each other in a natural hot spring at the top of the world. Her long, wet, black hair touched the small of her back. Her crystal blue eyes windowed the joy in her heart. The smile on her face unveiled that little girl who always knew that she was born to be a pioneer. This is one of my life's most treasured memories.

*****

The hitchhikers *and* the sign shooters we met at this time had at least one thing in common—an insatiable hunger for freedom— the kind that can only be experienced when there are few or no enforceable rules. That hunger was just as essential a part of the psychological makeup of the thousands of workers who had left their homes and families to work on the Trans-Alaska pipeline (which in 1975 was two years from completion) as it was for the tribe of permanently restless wayfarers we would meet in this still wild corner of the continent.

If there had been a viable road that connected the north and south poles, Theresa and I would have hitchhiked to the top and bottom of the planet. And so would every one of the full-time wanderers we were bunking with on our longer-than-expected layover in the youth hostel on the road to more road in Whitehorse, Yukon.

In centuries to come, if manned space flights can be accessed by hitchhiking, the kind of people we met at this hostel will be interplanetary travelers because the earth is not large enough to contain or satisfy their wanderlust.

The city of Whitehorse sits at mile 918 on the AlCan highway. There were 22,000 people in the entire Yukon Territory when we were there. Whitehorse was home to roughly 70 percent of them.

Patience and faith were as essential to our survival as food, water, and the ability to stay warm. We were now months and thousands of miles into a life over which we had very little control. We knew it might take a while for a dirt-road Samaritan to lift us up and carry us forward to Alaska from this isolated waystation of the incurably restless. But hell, we had once waited for four hours on the Indio on-ramp before we caught a ride.

Standing beside the highway across from the youth hostel from 9:00 AM till 9:00 PM on day one was a bit of a test, but we had peanut butter and jelly sandwiches, so no prob.

On day two at the nine-hour mark we ran out of bread. So we feasted on peanut butter and jelly à la finger. No prob.

On day three at noon, we were eating dry rye flakes with jelly. Around 4:00 two drunk local guys were down in a gully near us. They were sharing the contents of a bottle in a paper bag and discussing details about a guy they had stabbed and left under a bridge.

Hmmm. If we were ever going to reach the limit to our patience and faith, the combination of being within earshot of this conversation, standing beneath yet another shotgun-blasted road sign (I don't believe we saw a single sign after we passed Dawson Creek, British Columbia that was still readable), and the fact that we couldn't sleep because the sun never went down, might just do it.

Exhausted, malnourished, and sleep-deprived, we walked a quarter mile down the road to put a little distance between us and the local true-crime miniseries. The only thing we could do then was wait.

Many things we learned during this time influenced how we navigated the challenges of the world in the decades that followed—practical things like how not to waste food and water, how to take a tube of toothpaste and roll it up from the bottom to squeeze out one last gob ... and then to unroll it and cut it open with your pocketknife to scrape out the last brushable vestiges. But the lesson of staying calm, being observant, having faith, and not making a difficult situation that you have no control over more difficult has proven to be the most valuable and enduring. Thank you, *three days in Whitehorse*, for giving us no choice but to learn to be attentive, calm, and hopeful in high-stress situations. It sucked, but it is a lesson that has paid us innumerable dividends for nearly fifty years.

At the twelve-hour mark of day three, because, like supplies, everything takes longer to get to the top of the world, our angel in a beat-up 1968 Jeep finally arrived. Theresa sat in the back with our bag of dry rye flakes on her lap. I sat in the front. And off toward Alaska we did ride.

When it started to rain the driver pointed to a small crank handle he had installed on the inside frame beside the windshield and informed me that I could repay him for the ride by turning it. When I did, I learned that it was connected to the windshield wipers. We rode the next eleven hundred miles in an old jeep with homemade manual windshield wipers. It was heaven.

Alaska

Back in Alberta one of the woodsmen/survivalist/freedom-from-rules-and-regulations/bearded brethren had given us a book on wild edible plants. By the time we got to Alaska our meals were almost always supplemented with food we found in the wild. There was an edible mushroom that grew everywhere. We would gather a few and pick some lamb's quarters, cut off some of the onion and turnip we had bought for twenty-five cents and cook it all in a pan over a small fire. This is who we were now. This is how we lived. I remember savoring the taste of these meals the way I would the chef's special in a trendy, overpriced restaurant today. We didn't stop supplementing our diet with lamb's quarters (also called pigweed and wild spinach) till we stopped hitchhiking in November of 1979.

As much as I loved our twenty-five cent dinners, I didn't miss them the day we purchased a freshly caught salmon from a native Alaskan. It cost two dollars. (The price of eight pigweed/turnip stir-fries.) But the extravagance was made more palatable when he threw in a three-pound cod for free. We fed the entire campground that day.

We hitchhiked every major road in Alaska—Anchorage to Fairbanks and then out to Chena Hot Springs. We met all sorts of wild people and heard countless stories about how not to die in subzero temperatures. And how Fairbanks has the worst air pollution in the United States in the winter because the cold keeps all the wood smoke from people's homes from dissipating and no one shuts their car off all winter. And how more people own planes in Alaska than in any other state in the union because most of the state is accessible only by water or air.

Our last stop was Mount McKinley (which has since been given back its original name Denali).

The one thing we knew when we left Lynn was that we wanted to get as far away from that place as possible. The lack of a passport and an amount of cash beyond what was required to simply maintain minimum sustenance imposed firm limitations on that goal. At Mount McKinley we were six hundred miles from the Bering Strait. There was no more road. In early August of 1975 we learned that the answer to the question how far away from Lynn can you hitchhike in North America was exactly four thousand five hundred and sixty-six point three miles.

The road had far exceeded its promise to expand our view of the world and our potential. In half a year we had gone from getting drunk with our friends on gallons of two-dollar wine to dining on wild edible plants at the top of the continent.

We knew this was a turning point. After visiting this mountain, we were going to take all we had learned and *turn* back toward all that we had come from. We had entered the National Park under a cloud of poignancy.

The thing we heard the most about Mount McKinley was that, because of its height of over twenty thousand feet and other meteorological factors, the peak was almost always cloud-covered.

We spent an entire day on a bus tour through the park. We saw a triple rainbow. (Which we were sure was placed there by the universe to acknowledge how far we had journeyed and how much we had grown.) Then, far off in the distance, we saw what we were sure was a yellow pickup truck. While we were speculating on the advanced level of driving skills one would need to navigate through all the brush and rocks between us and the location of the truck, we saw it move. The big yellow pickup turned its head and stared at us. After confirming that we weren't having a mutual psychedelic flashback, we realized that what we were seeing was a grizzly bear. Please believe me when I tell you that I do not want to spend another minute of my life talking about bears. But ... let me say this one last thing. No Jasper brown bear could ever be mistaken for a pickup truck. Male Alaskan grizzlies weigh 1,700 pounds. Their heavyweight champion status is undisputed. And no one has a clearer understanding of this fact than a comparatively dainty nine-hundred-pound Jasper brown bear. And ... be assured that if ever your hanging bottles should be clinked by one of them your calls for the bear dog will go unheeded.

We didn't know it, but our triple rainbow indicated that the clouds were lifting and, sure enough, the entire twenty-thousand-three-hundred-and-ten-foot-high mountain was revealed. I pictured Theresa and I standing on its snow-covered peak at night and touching the moon.

*****

The invincibility we felt at the beginning of our travels originated from a lack of knowledge. What we didn't know about the world back then would have filled all the pages in the library. Invincibility was just one of several uninformed delusions we had embraced.

But as we headed south from Alaska, our fearlessness was based in the fact that we had survived so much. We had become well aware of our mortality, having eyeballed it up close on several occasions, but unlike our earlier incarnation we were now armed with survival skills, experience, a track record, and an unshakable (albeit naive) belief in the inherent benevolence of the universe.

Whenever we had less than five dollars on hand, we would leave it at the base of an on-ramp road sign. We could get by for a long time without money as long as we had a good supply of beans and rice. We felt an obligation to let the next kindred spirits who came along know that the universe was watching out for them. There was something freeing about giving away our last few bucks to someone we would never meet. It was just a small way of paying it forward and reinforcing our belief that we would be just fine for the week or so until more money arrived. (It's important to state here that we would have been less likely to part with our last few dollars if it were really our last few dollars. There is a limit to the amount of trust that even cosmic, triple rainbow, be-here-now sages in training are willing to hand over to the universe.)

I'll Be Fine Without You

The first of the stories with which I will conclude this history of our freshman hitchhiking year is one that I hope will clarify the possible misconception that may have arisen in the minds of some readers that Ms. Theresa and I spent all of 1975 without expressing a harsh word in the direction of one another. We got along extraordinarily well considering that we spent every day for close to twelve months without any time apart. But come on now. Take a good long look at your soul mate and picture spending every minute of 360 consecutive days together. Don't feel bad about the thoughts you're having. That amount of unrelieved companionship would test the patience of Mahatma Gandhi, Mother Teresa, and the mellowest of all the stoned-to-the-bone hippies who ever lived.

Before we venture to the southern coast of British Columbia, let's jump ahead to central Oregon. The coasts of Washington and Oregon have an entirely different feel than their central and eastern regions.

On the coasts it was common for folks to pull over and say,

"we don't have room but here's a few bucks" or "smoke this, it'll help pass the time." Away from the coasts these types of interactions were less frequent. People were nice enough, but we always noticed that the number of pickup trucks chucking beer cans out the window at us ticked up a bit away from the Pacific.

One day we were in a palpably uncomfortable part of the state on a lonesome back road. We were bickering. In mid-argument Theresa hoisted her pack onto her back, walked across the road, and began hitchhiking in the opposite direction.

I immediately pictured myself sitting with her parents saying, "I haven't seen her since I pissed her off and she took a ride from the next car that came along." This was a think-quick moment. I didn't know much, but I was sure that the chances of the next driver not scooping her up were pretty slim. I imagined myself standing alone watching her fade into the sunset.

Whoa!

"I'm sorry. I'm sorry. You're right. I'm wrong. Please come back." Then, with a look that said, "I love you, but I will be just fine without you," she crossed back to my side of the road. The man who later gave us a ride, and I'm not making this up, told us that they had just found two murdered hitchhikers off the side of the road near where we had been standing.

Lasqueti Island

In Alaska we had camped with a woman who lived on Vancouver Island. During a discussion of how far we had all ventured to satisfy our desire to experience the world the way it was before our time, she suggested that we visit Lasqueti Island. It was, she said, a small island off the coast of Vancouver Island that was inhabited by a tribe of the most fiercely off-the-grid hippies on earth.

It was mid-September when we boarded the ferry from Vancouver Island to Lasqueti. Calling this tiny, barely motorized, glorified rowboat a ferry indicated to us that the residents of this island had a playful sense of humor.

The sun was setting as we disembarked the wee ferry. We were struck by the fact that there was nothing near the dock. No store. No houses—just a small wooden wharf with ocean on one side and woods on the other. We began walking down the only road (dirt, of course) and looking for a place to set up the tent before dark. Within five minutes the same bully rainstorm that had been scouring the continent for us since we left Boulder spotted my orange backpack and reinitiated its merciless attack on our well-being.

It poured. We were instantly and thoroughly drenched. There didn't seem to be any place near us that was open or flat enough to set up the tent. Then we spied a small patch of grass by the side of the road. It was just big enough. In these days we could set up our shelter in three minutes. At minute number one we realized that the grass was growing in a half inch of soil that was on top of solid rock. I was using a stone to try to pound the metal tent pegs into what I thought was soil, only to watch them bend in half. Finally, we splashed our asses down in a big puddle and burst into laughter.

The deluge was so severe that we couldn't even put the tent back inside its carrying sack. We just rolled it up like it was a giant joint. I held one end and she the other. It swung between us as we walked down the road completely defenseless against the torrential rain and laughing like crazy people. Then, like even crazier people, we started singing Grateful Dead songs and kept walking … toward who knows what.

Within the thunder we could hear the big deep male voice of the storm trying to strike fear into our hearts and get us to panic. It had lots of reverb and echo on it for dramatic effect.

Boooom! "You have no shelter, shelter, shelter-rrr. I am the mighty wind and rain and I'm going to kill you, you, yooou." *Boooom!* "Cell phones won't be made available to the public for nine more years, years, yeeaarrs. You could not be more alone or wet or vulner-able, able, able." *Boooom! Lightning! Boooom!*

There was no panic in us. We tried to set up shelter. We failed. What now? Laugh. Sing. Walk back to the dock and stand under it to get out of the rain and then see what happens. Something will happen.

The first and only person we saw that evening appeared to us like a vision through the downpour. (Perhaps he was a Grateful Dead fan and the sound of our rain-soaked harmonies summoned him forth.) He said, "Me and my friend are spending the night in an abandoned church down the road. Come on."

Every single panic-worthy situation that we found ourselves at the mercy of in the past year had been resolved with kindness from strangers. We navigated this one with calm and humor and faith and song. We embraced the moment—the wet, stupid moment—like two sages who had finally learned to apply their Zen lessons.

"Congratulations Grasshoppers, you have passed the test, test, tessstt." *Booom! Lightning! Boooom!*

The next day in the bright sunshine we hitched to an abandoned orchard that our new friends had told us about. The car we got a ride in had no hood and no doors. That was a first. Getting an automobile on to the island was a very expensive endeavor. Keeping the motor in working condition was the only thing that mattered to the owners of Lasqueti's tiny fleet of ugly vehicles. Hoods and doors were optional and considered luxuries.

It was mid-September. The fruit was ripe. We feasted on

blackberries and pears and then discovered that there were oysters on the rocks by the ocean at the edge of the property.

We knew that this first year of our adventuring was winding down. A harvest of fruit and seafood seemed a fitting banquet to celebrate all we had accomplished, not only in miles traveled but also in allowing the road to permanently alter the way we saw our place in the world ... and the trajectory of our lives.

The Painted Desert Incident

For the next six weeks we sauntered around the west. We visited our friends in Colorado, California, and Arizona. We stayed longer. We drank deeper of their company and were more present during conversations. Traveling was no longer about getting to the next further-away place. We were done with that. We were refining and customizing our approach to travel. From this point forward it was going to be about learning, listening, and growing. These weeks foreshadowed the slower pace, deeper dive, let's-stay-here-until-it-feels-like-time-to-go strategy that we would employ during our adventures in 1977 and 1979.

We were getting weary. Eleven months of sleeping on the ground and hitchhiking tens of thousands of miles will give an eighteen-year-old body a taste of what fifty feels like. Money was running out. Winter was coming. All signs pointed to going home to regroup and see if we had stayed away long enough for the new Don and Theresa to not fall back into becoming the old Don and Theresa. This thought weighed on us as September gave way to October.

We had just finished a short walking tour of the Petrified Forest National Park in Arizona. We were about to cross interstate 40 to head east toward New Mexico when a van passed us and pulled over a long distance down the road. It then backed up a hundred yards or so and stopped. Two very large, hairy men emerged and began running toward us.

Desolate is an entirely inadequate word to describe the middle-of-nowhere-ness of that stretch of highway. I thought, "this could be it. This could be the moment that people in every state warned us about. These guys are huge. I weigh 110 pounds. We're screwed." As they got closer, they seemed to get bigger and hairier and scarier. "Thousands of rides with strangers. Tens of thousands of miles travelled to the far edges of the continent, and this is how it ends? Killed in the desert. No one to witness how it happened. Bodies never found. A tragically cliché ending to an amazing story that no one will ever be told. Damn."

The two men slowed down as they got closer to us. I had my hand on my folding knife, which I had opened and was concealing in my pocket. The tension was building. Then one of the men yelled … Don and Theresa!

They were two of our friends from Lynn.

They cooked some soup on a Coleman stove. We ate lunch. They went west. We went east.

It was time to go home.

Part 2

Welcome Home

A week after the end of our first year of travel, I attended a house party in Lynn.

Theresa and I were taking a well-earned break from each other's company, so I went alone.

I was excited to reunite with my old schoolmates and friends and anxious to tell them about my adventures.

The guy who was throwing the party was a member of my high school graduating class. As I approached the house, he was leaning over a four-foot picket fence and puking into his mother's flower garden.

"Hey John, how you doing?" "Huh? Oh, hi Don, I'll be all right in a minute. There's a keg in the bathtub. Have at it." As he recommenced the spraying of his special blend of homemade plant food over his mother's daffodils, I entered the party … and the world I had left behind.

There they were—the people who had grown up like me. They were doing what came natural—drinking, smoking weed, and talking about hockey. The J. Geils Band *Bloodshot* album was blaring track number one, "(Ain't Nothin' but a) House Party," from the turntable inside John's Mom's stereo console.

When the needle had reached the end of side one and the subtle musical stylings of our favorite local crooners had ended, I heard a sound I hadn't been in the presence of for over a year. But one I recognized instantly. It was the sound of knuckles striking a cheek bone.

Two of the king's most loyal and chivalrous warriors were

engaged in a valiant duel for the affections of a fair maiden whose virtue had apparently been maligned. Furniture was upended. Precious hops and barley were spilled. The face of the young woman (that may have launched a thousand ships) got collaterally damaged after she inserted it, in an ill-advised peacekeeping effort, between the combatants. This, I felt, ensured that, despite their willingness to die defending her honor, neither of these noblemen would win the lady's hand and acquire the highly revered title of her betrothed.

I leaned against the wall and watched the familiar scene unfold. The rest of the guests moved instinctively away from the action and continued their discussions about the Boston Bruins as if nothing was going on.

With a grin on my face that acknowledged how out of place I was, I imagined the looks of bewilderment my road stories about dinners of fresh picked wild lamb's quarters in Alaska would manifest, if I were fool enough to tell them here. Then, as I finished my beer, I whispered to an imaginary, non-vomiting host, "Thanks, but I'll let myself out."

Welcome home little wanderer.

*****

The first coming home lesson, as we just learned, was that I needed to keep my stories to myself—which I did. From everyone.

Most people who yearn for adventure are denied the opportunity by job and family obligations. Laying unsolicited stories of boundless freedom upon their kitchen tables is insensitive at best.

But the main reason for keeping these stories under lock and key for decades was my ever-growing respect and appreciation for people who worked at unfulfilling jobs without complaining.

They coached their kid's hockey teams. They did all the step-by-step, day-to-day things that gave their families a chance for a better life ... and they never complained. I, on the other hand, whined and moaned about everything, and had yet to meet a responsibility that I didn't consider running away from. I had no intention of starting my seemingly inevitable thirty-year stint in the factory before all my other options were exhausted. But I knew at this time that the selfless commitment and dogged determination to do the right thing for the future of loved ones that most folks embraced was noble and difficult and honorable—so, "Stop being a dick and shut up about your wild times on the road Don White."

*****

The bony, outstretched, tentacles of unsatisfying employment (which I complained about incessantly) celebrated my return by delivering me to the working world via a job as a busboy at an upscale restaurant.

I rented an apartment with a friend next to the General Electric Factory where the steady hum of a million motors served as a constant reminder that I had returned to the heart of industrial America.

1976 worked tirelessly to diminish the power of my memories of freedom and my belief that I needn't succumb to a life of quiet desperation.

It took away my willingness to share what I had learned.

It planted me next to a 24/7 industrial hum.

It dressed me in a red vest and a bow tie.

And, just to be mean, it found me a job cleaning up the slop left on white linen tablecloths by the kind of insufferable rich people who for all of 1975 had driven past me in their mobile homes while the elements tried to kill me.

I knew I was up against a formidable adversary.

But I had gone too far and been away too long. This was not the first time my intestinal fortitude had been underestimated. I wasn't going to surrender without a fight.

Utilizing my life's diligently acquired and well-worn tools of resistance to the status quo, I initiated the following defensive maneuvers and counterpunching techniques.

I limited my associates to a small group of friends who had experienced the world beyond the city limits.

I started regular jam sessions with local musicians.

I took advantage of the fact that Lynn was close to the People's Republic of Cambridge and Harvard Square—the most progressive two-mile stretch of land on the East Coast—by visiting there as often as possible.

I hitchhiked short distances just to stay in shape and glimpse the life I was defending.

I stopped going to John's parties.

And … most importantly, me and my band of besieged free spirits became unapologetic Grateful Dead heads.

Of all the counter punches I employed to resist and survive the spirit-crushing forces of humiliating employment, and the constant pressure to be satisfied with my one year of freedom and to "make something of myself," being among the easy-to-mock fans of that band from San Francisco was the most effective.

Every Dead show that I attended that year was a traveling, distilled assemblage of the kind of people that drew me to and kept me on the road. It was like Big Sur crammed into a concert hall. These events were an essential recharging station for me. In their afterglow the donning of my red servant's vest only strengthened my resolve to stay focused, save money, and look ahead to the day when I could turn in my black bow tie and hit the road again.

1977

There were many things about Theresa that impressed me when we first became boyfriend and girlfriend in early 1974. But nothing fascinated me more than her uncompromising independence. In those early days we would enter a house party together. Once inside, I would turn left, and she would turn right. We would each spend the entire night separated from each other and talking with our friends. When it was time to go, we would reconnect and leave together.

I know that many men are insecure and possessive about their girlfriends (especially when she is gorgeous and cooler than other girls and you know that every boy at the party wants her). But I have always been wired the opposite way. I have no interest in influencing the decision making of anyone I am with. I will be making my own decisions. They are always free to do the same. At the instant any girlfriend or potential girlfriend or girl I was with at an event expressed displeasure about who I was talking to at a party, I would start composing the words I would be using to tell her that it wasn't working out and that I was moving on. I am not insecure. I am fiercely independent.

Meeting this teenager who grew up in federal housing and had seen so much real-world drama that at fourteen she was more grown up than most people in their twenties—who had zero tolerance for being told what to do and was more fiercely independent than me—was like hitting the lottery. I didn't know how many women like this existed. But I knew they were hard to come by.

Theresa and I were nineteen years old when we came off the road at the end of 1975. We had spent every single minute of that year together. No one would think that the relationship of two teenagers could survive that or, if by some miracle it did, that they shouldn't spend a little time apart.

I knew from our first kiss that I wanted to grow old with her. If I thought about all the other women I knew or could get to know (which I did because, duh, I was eighteen), I could and did imagine all kinds of fun things, but growing old with them wasn't one.

When we visited our friends in rural communities in Maine and elsewhere it was not uncommon to meet or hear about a woman in her mid-thirties who married her first or second boyfriend at eighteen, realized it was a mistake, then dumped her husband and hit the party circuit to grab some of those uninhibited wild times that her friends had when they were in their twenties.

If Theresa decided to go the distance with me, I wanted her decision making to have been free of my influence for more than a year. Her independent streak was a key ingredient of what separated her from everyone else for me. I knew that it had yet to exert its potential free from the influence of others. For her to go through all the ups and downs of a long life with me it would be best if she could look back and know that, if given the opportunity, her uninfluenced decision making could be trusted. I wanted a partner who knew she could make it without me. Nothing else would do.

We each got our own apartments. Giving each other space was not a hard sell after all that time together. There probably was nothing that could have stopped it from happening.

We didn't disappear from each other's lives. We were together quite often. But our personal decisions were our own.

After a few months I remember thinking, "This is the stupidest plan for winning the woman of your dreams that has ever been hatched in the entire history of human relations. Think about how desirable she is. Everybody wants her. Think about how many men there are who are more interesting than you—who have money and can open up parts of the world to her that you can't."

But after these moments of quiet panic, I would always come back to a few things that I felt strongly about. The dialogue in my mind would go like this.

How much do you love her?

More than anything I've known, heard about, or can imagine.

Do you trust her judgment?

Yes.

Is your love for her and your trust in her judgment big enough to accept the fact that she may decide that there is someone out there that is better for her to grow old with?

That one stung.

But I always came back to this: Who loves a woman more? Is it the guy who believes that if she experiences some of the world without him that he will lose her and then works to limit her potential out of fear and insecurity? Or is it the guy who says, "I love this woman and trust her judgment. I want her to fulfill every aspect of her potential and if she then decides to grow old with someone else, I'll be devastated but eventually I'll find comfort in knowing that my love for her was big enough to put her long-term happiness above my loss."?

Seriously, the stupidest way of all time to try to keep a woman.

But I must say that, even though I couldn't think of one relationship that survived anything similar, I knew it wasn't out of the question. We had hitchhiked to Alaska and had experiences that could not be matched by anyone. I didn't just want her. I wanted a version of her that did lots of living without me so she wouldn't be longing to recapture those years under the pressures of a long relationship. I also knew that to go the distance all the way to being an elderly couple, that it had to be her decision. It was a long shot for sure. But I knew I had a chance.

In October of 1976 Theresa and another young woman left Lynn for a hitchhiking adventure of an intentionally undetermined duration.

She returned in mid-February of 1977.

For a few months prior to the beginning of her four-month hitchhiking adventure with her friend, Theresa and I had been in each other's company with increasingly less frequency. We still had the same circle of friends, but we'd been off the road for nine months and were settling into a less connected life with each other.

She had let go of her apartment when she left. So when she came back in February she stayed with me. I told her that I planned to hitchhike by myself from March through June in New England. And that, come July, if she was interested, that I would love to hit the road with her again.

She was non-committal.

*****

Using the money I saved from the tips of wealthy restauranteurs, I upgraded all my weathered camping gear. In early March I loaded up my new backpack and hitched to Acadia National Park near Bar Harbor, Maine.

I wanted to be alone on the road for a while.

The year I had spent in my hometown had taught me to appreciate the strength of the forces that were opposing my return to the vagabond life. I knew this was a war they would eventually win and that I would have to make the best of that workaday life once it could no longer be evaded. This knowledge gave me a sense of urgency and forced me to focus on accelerating the speed of my personal growth. To that end, I carried with me several books about philosophy and religion. I also brought a notebook for journaling.

Hypothermia licked her frosty lips when she saw me setting up camp near the rocky coast of Maine with February still visible in the rearview mirror. When her attempts to freeze me to death were casually brushed away by my fancy new camping equipment, her disappointment was palpable.

Throughout this period I kept getting a sneaking suspicion, an unfounded, ludicrous notion, that I might possibly be showing faint early signs of becoming a man. I dug clams with improvised tools and cooked them for dinner every day. I read books by Joseph Campbell and Carlos Castaneda. And in my journal, I wrote songs and stories and poetry and letters to my better self.

My Dearest Better Self,

I'm sorry for locking you in the basement and ignoring your advice for all these years. I'm hoping we can make up and begin anew on the job of molding me into the kind of man I can someday be proud of. I realize that from where we stand today the goal seems a trifle optimistic. But in my defense, three days ago several people lost the office pool when I lived to celebrate my twentieth birthday. I understand that this one event does not make twenty-one a riskier bet in the next pool. It could however, to those visionaries like yourself who still believe in miracles, be viewed as a glimmer of hope and an indication of potential.

If my ability to envision my future were all it took to manifest it, I (we?) could rest easy. The me I hope to be is becoming more clearly formed in my mind with each passing day. I've seen enough of the world now to know that there are many things I learned during my working-class upbringing that I value and want to include in the makeup of the new breed of brickyard/hippie hybrid I'm hoping you'll help me become.

If together we can use these next months to accelerate my personal and spiritual growth without losing these working-class qualities, I believe the best of both worlds is possible.

Please advise.

Yours truly,
Donnie White

*****

The people I met between March and June while hitching all around Maine, Vermont, western Massachusetts, and New Hampshire were northern New England versions of the west coast hippies that we were drawn to in 1975—interested in many of the same things but genetically adapted to show an unforgiving winter the respect it deserves. They were hearty, work ethic-y homesteaders, organic farmers, and back-to-the-landers. Not a lot of staring at the warm ocean from hot springs and pondering higher levels of consciousness with these folks. There was work to do. Potato planting. Wood chopping. Barn building. Can't be lazy. Winter is coming.

I stayed with many of the people who picked me up and absorbed whatever they were willing to teach me. Then I would hike alone on the Long Trail in Vermont or the Appalachian Trail in New Hampshire and Maine. I felt a kinship with Thoreau and all the other outsiders who needed time alone in nature to focus their thoughts. I knew who I wanted to be. These four months solidified the vision in my mind.

Sometime in June, after twenty months of making her own decisions and having her own adventures, Theresa informed me by phone that if the offer was still on the table, she would meet up with me in July and we could take to the road again together.

I was staying at a friend's house in Maine. When I hung up the phone, he saw a look on my face that he couldn't interpret. It was the face of a thousand emotions. He asked me if I was okay? I said, yes, and went outside. As I stood beneath the stars, I felt like crying. For months I had been preparing myself to deal with the reality that Theresa was probably going to grow old with someone else—that too much time had gone by—and that for the rest of my life I would question my decision and regret the fact that I didn't fight to keep her the way any sane man on earth would have done.

I had already pictured myself congratulating her on her wedding day and wondering if I would ever be the kind of man that could be genuinely happy that she found the person that was perfect for her.

Standing in the yard I recalled a memory from my childhood. I was eight. Our dog had escaped from the animal shelter where we had left him while we were on vacation. I was a little boy who had lost his dog. I was devastated. I thought for sure he would find his way back to me. My parents let me believe that, but even at eight years old I knew that they thought he was never coming back.

At night I would dream that I saw him running down the street toward our house. I knew he'd never stopped trying to get back home to me. I would be hugging him and he'd be licking my face and wagging his tail and we would run home and tell my parents. And I would say, "I always knew he would come back to me. And he did, Mom! Look, my puppy came home to me … because he loves me!"

And then I would wake up.

Standing beneath a billion stars that night I just knew I was going to wake up. This had to be a dream. She was already gone. My plan had failed. I was eight months into getting used to the idea that our lives would move forward in the arms of others.

Two weeks later at a trailer on some farmland in another part of Maine, I was sitting on a cinder block that was unsuccessfully masquerading as a front doorstep when a car drove up the long dirt road and stopped in front of me. Theresa got out of the back seat, pulled her backpack out of the trunk, and laid it on the ground. The car drove away. And she stood there.

Although this woman had a strong resemblance to the girl I had hitchhiked to Alaska with, to my eye she was an entirely different person.

I had seen her five months earlier and quite frequently before she hit the road in October. But I had trained my mind to not think about how magnificent she was because I knew she had slipped away and it would only crush me to do so.

But in this moment my mind withdrew its protective barrier and let me gaze upon her as the woman of my dreams—who had experienced the wide world for twenty months and decided that I was the man she wanted to build a life with.

The first difference was physical. I had travelled to Alaska with a teenager. Standing before me now was a woman. Teenagers are cute. Women are beautiful. There is no comparison. To me they are almost like different species. There wasn't an ounce of fat on her but somehow her body was subtly fuller in the areas that emphasize the differences between the youthful and the mature.

The second difference was the confidence. I could see it emanating from the way she carried herself. When she began to walk toward me, her self-assurance, her self-esteem, and her pride, became more commanding with every step. She looked invincible.

I still thought I was going to wake up and realize my puppy wasn't coming home, but I didn't. I just sat there wide awake and thinking that standing here before me is everything I ever wanted—a partner to adventure with for the rest of my life—who chose me over everyone else and who exuded the confidence of an empress.

I could describe every detail of how we made love that night because I can remember every second of it like it happened yesterday. But Theresa says that's none of your business. I said, "What if they pay double for the book?" She said, "Nope." Sorry.

However, let me prompt your imagination so you can create your own version.

My dream version of my dream woman had just fallen back into my arms after I was sure she had been forever lost to me. I was one grateful dude. I planned to express my gratitude in a manner that, come morning, would leave no doubt that choosing me was a wise decision.

How would I accomplish that, you ask?

I would devote my slow, steady, loving attention to every part of her, including, but not limited to, her temples and the tips of all her fingers. There would not be a single inch of her left unworshipped. I would be slow and focused. And, ever so gradually, I would build and then release the tension until all her fires were raging. In essence, I would love her with a passion and attention to detail that was worthy of the only woman who could make my dreams come true ... and had just decided to do so.

It would take hours.

If the next person you lie beside treats you with ten percent of the love and attentiveness that happened in Maine that night, I promise you will remember every second of it for the rest of your life.

The next day we decided that Newfoundland might make for a nice little jaunt.

Newfoundland

Theresa and I crossed from Maine into New Brunswick, Canada in early July of 1977. We spent the entire month in Nova Scotia. The connections between Boston and that lovely province are long and deep. Strands of both our ancestries have their North American origins there.

At the time we didn't have a full appreciation of the fact that we were tracing the steps of those in our bloodline who crossed the Atlantic and started new lives in the upper eastern regions of this continent.

According to oral family history, my father's father came to Lynn from a place called Digby, Nova Scotia with his dad and brothers in the early 1900s. They were carpenters and made their living building houses.

The Pothier side of Theresa's family came from France and settled in the town of Wedgeport. Nova Scotia felt like home to us. This feeling was reinforced by the fact that many of the people we met there looked like they could be our relatives. At first it was exciting. But after a couple of weeks being surrounded by strangers who looked like our cousins and aunts and uncles, began to feel like a weird (kinda creepy) dream.

We took the ferry from North Sydney, Nova Scotia to Port aux Basques, Newfoundland. We found a lot of dirt roads there with an astonishing number of drunk people driving at high speeds on them. Seriously, it would be much quicker for me to list and describe the rides where the driver wasn't drinking than to document the ones where there was a bottle of Labatt Blue in the driver's hand and a near-empty sixpack beside him on the front seat. It was as if, in Newfoundland, when each new car left the showroom, it was given a year's supply of Canadian-made beer.

When we asked an old man who picked us up if it was always this cold in July he said, "You missed summer. It was Tuesday." We asked him if he knew of any place where it would be okay for us to set up our tent near the ocean. He looked at us like we had asked him if there was any place nearby where we could find air to breathe. This was Newfoundland in the seventies. The concept of having to worry about being chased off someone's land hadn't quite taken hold yet. He just waved his arm out the window and said, "There." He was shaking his head when he let us out. "Where can you find a place by the ocean to camp in Newfoundland? Americans just keep getting dumber."

We hiked up to a big flat field. At its northern edge were rocky cliffs that were nearly as impressive as Ireland's Cliffs of Moher. We spent three days staring at the ocean and thinking about how we both had the leave-it-all-behind-cross-the-Atlantic-start-a-new-life-in-someplace-where-winter-is-king blood in us.

Early on the second day we watched a man in a tiny boat row northward until the horizon absorbed him. Five hours later he reappeared. Maybe it wasn't as dangerous and strenuous as it seemed. Maybe it was normal for men in this part of the world to spend the entire day alone paddling out on the North Atlantic. But I couldn't help but wonder what it said about a person's marriage when, rather than spend the day with your spouse, you choose instead to row your dinghy to Greenland.

The Atlantic Ocean. It connected us to the people from whom we were descended. It was the watery beast that stood between all of them and their dreams of a better life. Within

Theresa and I there is not a trace of blood from Europeans who played it safe. Everyone from the mid-eighteen-hundreds on who contributed to our genetic makeup looked at this ocean, fully aware of all the souls it had pulled forever to its depths, and said, "I don't know what's on the other side or if I will live to see it, but I'm sure it will be better than here. So fuck it, I'm going."

I'm probably going to call this story "The Hitchhiking Years." But "Fuck It, I'm Going" is a very tempting title.

Theresa's grandfather was one of only two survivors of a shipwreck near Germany when he was nineteen years old. His father was among the many souls lost at sea that day.

My maternal grandfather told me that in 1916 his father brought him to a dock in Greece, gave him twenty dollars and said get on that boat. There was a tremendous storm. It took weeks to get to Ellis Island. Several people died. My grandfather couldn't speak a word of English. He was sixteen years old.

We are descended from risk takers. Nova Scotia and Newfoundland made it clear to us that we didn't invent this idea of not fearing the unknown—we were made of it.

Just like in Alaska, we hitchhiked everywhere we could find a road that someone might possibly consider driving on. The furthest north we could get was a place called Eddie's Cove near the top of the Great Northern Peninsula. The rocks along the coast there were covered with what we thought were juniper bushes. Upon closer inspection we realized that they were pine trees that had grown up six inches from the ground and then bent sideways to hug the rocks. It was a powerful statement about the foolhardiness of standing upright in the face of the North Atlantic's winter winds. It was also a statement (and a bit of a reminder) about adapting and thriving under the oppression of an unrelenting adversary.

Across the strait of Belle Isle, we saw what we believed to be

Labrador. We really wanted to go there. I simply cannot express how badly we wanted to go to Labrador. It was right there! But, as far as we could tell, the establishment of a public ferry was decades away. And, although being a stowaway on a freighter sounded like a story that would tell well in the future, we eventually and reluctantly and with great disappointment in our hearts, decided against it.

Part 3

1978

We spent all of 1978 in Maine.
We lived with Theresa's brother and his wife.
We love them dearly.
They were extremely kind and patient with us.
We weren't easy.
They were trying to build a life and we were like geese looking at the sky hoping that each new day was the beginning of migration.

I held a series of horrible jobs.
I stayed at each one for as long as I could stand it.
The button factory.
The chicken canning plant.
The fiberglass canoe laminating shop.
The lobster trap assembly garage.

I cleaned out commercial chicken coops.
I pushed trash around the town dump in a bulldozer.

I paved driveways with some guys who were fresh out of jail.
I cut down trees.
And, of course, I dug clams.

Theresa and I got married in the field behind her brother's house in October.
We left for our final year of hitchhiking in November.

These are study notes. There will be a quiz on Friday.

Lijah

One attractive adult female flower child
One bearded and not especially attractive hippie dude
One gray sixty-pound backpack
One blue sixty-pound backpack
One mid-size golden retriever
One homemade saddle-bag-style dog backpack
One inexpensive and barely tunable guitar

We received no rides in VW beetles in 1979. You needed a moving van to pick us up.

Truth be told, U.S. auto makers had not yet developed an interest in fuel efficiency, so the insides of most cars were still cavernous and well able to accommodate our picturesque road family and our portable belongings.

Theresa wanted babies. Being the genius that I am, I bought her a female golden retriever to mollify her mothering instincts.

By Autumn of 1982, however, we not only had a dog but we also had two children.

Genius.

Back in 1979, insofar as the persistence of Theresa's biological clock was concerned, Lijah the hitchhiking dog could only postpone the inevitable. But within the context of making us the most irresistible ride solicitors on the Indio on-ramps of the world, her contributions were peerless, unprecedented, and invaluable.

We were taking this hitchhiking game to a new level. Our visuals were groundbreaking. Part of it was attitude. There was not a hint of desperation in us. We were not trying to get anywhere. Having previously explored the outer reaches of the continent, our disinterest in miles-for-the-sake-of-miles was absolute. This was going to be the year where we used what we had learned about this soon-to-become-obsolete mode of travel to seek out and spend time with bohemians.

The new, highly refined, image we presented to an unsuspecting driving public was the stuff of legend.

Hitchhiking with a golden retriever, if I do say so myself, was an *actual* stroke of genius. The number of people who passed us by because they didn't have enough room or didn't want dog stink on their upholstery was rendered inconsequential by the significant increase in the number of people who picked us up because our dog was so freakin' adorable.

She was a purebred golden retriever. This breed, more than any other, is associated in the minds of everyone who knows anything about dogs with being one of the friendliest, gentlest, and anxious-to-please canines in the world. Goldens are the dogs that dog lovers wish people could be. You may have a rottweiler or a pit bull that is just as gentle as the average golden, but the question in the mind of many motorists will be, "How do I defend myself from an attack by that dog while I'm driving?"

Most people could picture *our* dog napping beside their children.

At this time no one had ever seen a backpack on a dog.

Theresa invented the prototype. She built it on her grand-mother's 1940s Singer sewing machine. It had a strap that went under Lijah's head and two saddlebags that hung on each side of her back with an adjustable strap that attached the two bags beneath her belly. In it Lijah carried her dog food. When food got low, she carried our laundry.

To further exploit our understanding of the power of dog cuteness, we accessorized her fashion ensemble with a red bandana around her neck that we folded neatly into a triangular downward-facing point.

No less than a dozen people that year stopped, got out of their cars, took pictures of us, and then drove away. We grew to expect it. No problem. "We were hoping for a ride from someone more interesting anyway."

A dog meticulously accoutered for maximum adorableness. A friendly, smiling, guy strumming his guitar. And a gorgeous young woman playing hopscotch and popping her thumb out at you with a big smile as she stood on one foot at the end of her series of one, two, one, two, one, hops—we were presenting a fifteen-second play assiduously designed to coax smiles out of even the dourest of America's drivers.

It was downright Oscar-worthy.

Adolescent Zealot

Throughout this entire year, whenever we came upon an interesting community of people, we would linger there until we felt that we had gathered and processed all the knowledge the group was willing to extend in our direction. Sometimes it took weeks. Sometimes it took minutes.

We were full-time seekers. I was well-versed in the philosophical worldviews of my previous mentors like Mickey the line crew foreman. I was hoping that my suspicion that the world may have produced thinkers who brought a more nuanced approach to questions regarding the meaning of life was not unfounded.

I began by reading the teachings of Jesus, Buddha, Krishna, Allah, Zoroaster (yes, even Zoroaster).

I then tried to get my mind to make sense of what history's great Eastern philosophers had to contribute to the conversation—Lao Tzu, Confucius, Rumi (love me some Rumi.)

Of course, interspersed within my reading materials were books that detailed a more 1960s-style approach to obtaining one's spiritual awakening—*The Dharma Bums, The Electric Kool-Aid Acid Test*.

It all converged to make me obnoxious.

If you made the mistake of talking philosophy or religion or hippie culture with me in those days, within minutes your eyes would glaze over and you would feel a pressing need to effectuate a reason to be elsewhere.

Nobody likes a zealot. Not even other zealots. But a man must invest a few years of uninterrupted focus into the object of his zeal to consume enough information so that in time he can meld it with his other life experiences to become the interesting hybrid of his aspirations.

I think of these overzealous years as the gangly, uncomfortable, adolescence of my circuitous journey toward the ultimate acquisition of the watered down, barely qualifying, quasi-enlightenment that I am still seeking.

*****

While spending winter's coldest weeks in Tucson with Jim Powers we discovered an ashram where kundalini yoga and meditation techniques were practiced and taught.

We didn't know about kundalinis or kunda-anything. We "discovered" these people because they were serving free food. But we liked them. They were sweet and mellow and interesting. And most importantly, it didn't feel cult-y there. It felt cool. We were always comfortable with them.

Theresa was interested in learning as much as possible about yoga and meditation, so in line with our let's-see-what-kind-of-weird-shit-these-folks-are-into game plan, we attended a few lectures.

Kundalini meditation, we learned, is not a set of beliefs or a religion. Instead, it's a system for evoking energy inside yourself and developing mind-body awareness.

Cool.

These folks were not your run-of-the-mill teachers of rudimentary downward-facing-dog-level yoga poses. They journeyed much deeper. This became clear to me on the day I saw what I had to assume was a highly advanced practitioner slowly emerge from a long meditation.

At this point, dear reader, if I were to tell you that in my lifetime I have seen an extraordinary number of people who were stoned out of their minds, you'd believe me, right?

This dude put them all to shame. He was in a league of his own. He looked to be at that holy grail level of stoned to the bone that exists only in the mythology of those who dedicate their lives to its elusive acquisition. Whatever chakra he unleashed or awakening he awoke would have been worth five hundred bucks a dose if I could have supplied it to my friends back home in pill form.

Ashram. Kundalini. Dharma. Rumi. Lao Tzu. Enlightenment. Chakra. Zoroaster. Krishna. Buddha. Allah.

The words that appear in italics above the sentence you are now reading are this chapter's contributions to my ever-expanding list of things to not bring up at a keg party.

Taos

While passing through the San Francisco Bay Area that spring, we saw a sign on an overpass that said, "Where there is love, nothing is too much trouble. Abdul Baha."

Abdul who?

What kind of zealot spends hundreds of hours of reading about the world's religions and misses the entire Bahai faith and its seven million world-wide practitioners of peace and love? This was a serious blow to my ego and to how I perceived my place in the hierarchy of obnoxious spiritual pontificators.

*****

We had been warned not to go to Taos by a friend who had been robbed there. But during the six weeks we stayed in that mountain community our paltry belongings failed to draw the attention of any of the area's thieves.

The town had a cool feel. There was a head shop that had a bakery in it. I suspected that the inspiration for this two-pronged business venture appeared in a vision to the owners during a night of marijuana chain smoking.

"Dude, what if we start a headshop? No wait, listen to me. This will be awesome. So, we start a headshop and we sell water pipes and rolling papers. But wait, listen, we put signs everywhere that say all products are for tobacco use only ... *right?* But that's not the best thing. The best thing is we make it a bakery too! No, listen, this is the shit. We sell 'em their hookah. They'll get baked in the parking lot and then come back inside all wasted and satisfy their munchies by buying our homemade raspberry-filled donuts ... whoa."

In a corner of this stoner multiplex was a rack of used tie-dye shirts and hippie-girl dresses. You paid whatever you could afford. Theresa purchased another summer dress there. As soon as she put it on, we got a ride from Bob who was driving the most cliché of all the hippie mobiles ... you guessed it, a Volkswagen van. Bob's visuals did nothing to diminish—and actually served to reinforce—the stereotype. Let's describe him in the voice of my father. "He had the long hair and was wearing the hippie sandals that the girls with hairy legs wear." (Thanks Dad.) On the dashboard was a book called *Bahai Prayers* written by ... dah dah tah daah ... Abdul Baha.

I lived my whole life without ever hearing a word about this dude and he shows up twice in one week? Today I wouldn't even notice something like this but then, oh man, I knew it was a sign.

I told Bob, the hippiest of the hippies, that we had just heard about the Bahai faith and were hoping to learn more. He gave us the book and drove us to a campground where he introduced us to Raylea and Sola—two women in their forties who were meandering around the country and, of course, living out of a van.

If you're getting sick of hippie stories, this next section will make you want to kill yourself. Trust me.

Leaving home to live the destination-less life in our teens and twenties was like climbing through a window of opportunity before it was closed by the responsibilities of adulthood. Being in your forties and leaving your world behind to live that life was like throwing a chair through a window that closed twenty years ago and then climbing through it.

You could see the weight of their past on them. Etched into the lines on the faces of these two women were hard stories of love and loss. It was obvious to us that the lives they had left behind were complex and difficult.

We had a sense that meeting us and seeing the life we had chosen touched something in them that was connected to their back story. We loved them instantly. And they reciprocated that love with a depth of emotion that we certainly felt but that only they could fully know. In all our years of travel, the only time we ever felt mothered was during our weeks with Raylea and Sola.

Whatever they had been through had taught them that life was too short to stress out over. They were both stellar examples of the idea that every increase of stress and tension in a situation needs to be met with a proportional increase of calm. Nothing fazed them.

At night they would produce a bottle of whiskey and pour a half a shot into each of our cups of decaffeinated coffee. We would sip and talk. They taught us the art of savoring.

These women were more interested in dreams than anyone I met before or since. They were especially knowledgeable and practiced in the art of lucid dreaming. When I asked Ms. Raylea to explain it to me she said, "You know how sometimes during a dream you become aware that you are dreaming. Well, as soon as that happens, I say, if this is a dream then I can fly. I have a method where I start to run and pedal my legs like I am riding a bike. I do that until I lift off. So almost every night I consciously influence part of what happens in my dreams. And Don, dreaming is always more fun when you're flying."

Twenty-two-year-old fulltime seeker of cosmic secrets Don White could not have been more impressed with this.

One evening, over a cup of modestly whiskeyed decaf, I told her that I had been feeling ill for a few days and had been plagued by a reoccurring nightmare. "It always starts with me being chased by someone who is trying to hurt or even kill me. I feel like I am running for my life. Then I become stuck in mud and am unable to continue running. I never turn around to see who or what is chasing me. Then I wake up soaked in sweat and traumatized."

In a voice with a level of calm that was proportionally increased to meet my level of stress, she told me about a tribe of people who are extremely peaceful in their waking hours but extremely violent in their dream world. They teach their children to confront and fight and kill anyone who poses a threat to them in their dreams.

In all my dreams for weeks after acquiring this information, I was a vigilante. I took the law into my own hands. At the point where I'd be stuck in the mud, I would know it was a dream. I would then turn around, find a weapon in my hand, and shoot or bludgeon or chase away my enemy. The old nightmares ended with me waking up in a panic. These all ended with me walking away and telling someone how I had no choice but to do it—that I needed to justifiably homicide my dream villains.

Camp Cosmic

Every few days Bob's magic bus would appear and out would come some little wanderer that he had picked up and vetted for compatibility with our oasis of unconventional idea exploration.

There was Patrick, a twenty-year-old solo hitchhiker who, in the words of Frank Zappa, "could throw a mean tarot." He did readings for everyone.

Then Sunshine (yes, her name was Sunshine) who was into massage and reflexology.

One by one Bob was assembling an island of like-minded misfits of varying ages and backgrounds who were all pursuing a master's degree in advanced unorthodoxy.

Before long we were part of an unlikely community of twenty or so hand-picked seekers who would share and explore and sing and learn and rejoice together for what turned out to be a memorable and fleeting moment in time.

We had group meals every evening. Where did the food come from? Well … dumpster diving is such an indelicate term. Let's call it nutrition reclamation. The guy who worked the late shift at the hookah bakery would leave a bag of day-old pastries at the back door each night for us to bring to Camp Cosmic. The local food market had a cage with an unlocked gate where the employees would throw the produce they couldn't sell. Three bad grapes in a bunch—out. The outside of a head of lettuce a little wilted—throw it in the cage. We ate like royalty.

A couple of rules that all nutrition reclamationers must know: no meat under any circumstances and no potatoes no matter how good they look. Bad potatoes can and will kill you.

Two weeks into this scene and I was lucid-dreaming every night just daring someone to mess with me. There were banquets every evening. Each person that joined us on the wings of Bob's judgment was teaching us about things we had never heard of before. After-dinner conversations would continue to three or four in the morning. They were so compelling that despite the awesome vigilante adventures that awaited, I never wanted to leave the discussion to go to sleep. And then, of course, there were the group massage sessions.

Intrigued?

Of course you are.

I don't know whose idea it was to introduce this practice to our community. But I owe him or her a great big thank you.

One person lies on top of a picnic table. Ten people and their twenty hands gather around. Everyone picks a part of the person's body and concentrates on massaging it. Two hands working on your temples. Two on each foot. Two on each hand, massaging every finger. Someone on one shoulder, someone massaging the other and so on.

You know how sometimes a person that you like (we're excluding the similar moments initiated by creepy people) will walk up behind your chair and start massaging the muscles in your neck and shoulders? Reflect for a moment on how good you feel while it is happening and how you hope they'll never stop. Now imagine nine more people and eighteen more hands massaging all your stressed and strained muscles and pressure points at the same time.

Each muscle that is being massaged initiates a release of dopamine to your brain's pleasure centers. When twenty hands are massaging your body, your brain becomes so overloaded with happiness chemicals (or my preferred term organic joy juice) that it checks out and leaves you in a state of indescribable rapturous euphoria.

You haven't lived till you've experienced this.

One night at the peak of this period after food and massage

and music and amazing conversation, Theresa and I looked at each other and said, "We did it. We set out to find the things and people and ideas that were as far away from what we grew up around and here we are. Not only did we find it, but we helped to create a light so bright that it drew all the like-minded seekers to us." (That's the way we talked back then.)

The one thing you can be sure of with a gathering of wanderers is that in time they will wander. After a month or so the campground was back to its four original members.

A forest ranger came by one day and threw us out. "You can't live here." "Cool, but just to be clear, we can keep living, just not here, right? Okay, good to know. You want some day-old pastry?"

We packed up the van and drove high up into the mountains. We set up camp under the assumption that our ranger friend had given us tacit permission to live for a while longer, provided that we did so outside of his jurisdiction.

Reflexology. Lucid dreaming. Tarot. Abdul Baha. Bahai faith.

Water—Story One

During the early part of my 1977 solo travels, I had been hiking trails in the White Mountains of New Hampshire for a week. One afternoon I set up camp beside a mountain stream that fed into some waterfalls.

Around 5:00 that evening a group of inner-city middle-schoolers and their counselors arrived and began to set up for the night. They were part of a program called Outward Bound that brought urban kids into the woods to expand their worlds a bit.

That night, thirty minutes after everyone was in their sleeping bags, a question was hollered out from one of the tents. It featured a tone of annoyance that one might hear in the voice of a woman hollering out her bedroom window at the people next door because their music was too loud.

"Is that river gonna run all night?"

*****

Our new Taos campground was high in the Mountains. It was late spring. The snow on the thirteen-thousand-foot peaks was melting and the stream that ran beside our tent was twelve feet wide and rushing. Its constant roar was the audio backdrop for our time here.

During our earlier travels we never bought food that was perishable because we were always on the move. (After our peanut butter and granola fueled travels in 1975 the sight of either of those staples of road living would cause me emotional trauma. Peanut butter didn't cross my lips again till the nineties.) But this year was different. We had just spent every cent of the hundred dollars that my mom had mailed to General Delivery Taos, New Mexico on an assortment of cheeses, vegetables, and fruit.

We had devised what we thought was a brilliant method to keep our perishables refrigerated. We put them all in a green trash bag and tied the top into a knot so it was waterproof. Then we put the bag into a milk crate that our friends had been using for storage in their van. We placed it in the raging, roaring, frigid river and tied it to a tree.

The next day it was gone.

Our underestimating of Mother Nature had put us in a situation where we now had no food and no money. This provided us a good opportunity to test our ability to stay calm and optimistic under pressure.

We flunked the test. Fear and anxiety ruled our lives for a few hours. But then, after a walk through the woods and a reassessment of the situation, we hitchhiked to a payphone, called my mom (collect of course), and initiated the process of having another postal money order mosey across the country in the direction of our new settlement. We also stopped by the back of the produce market and did some emergency nutrition reclamation so we could eat that night.

As fate would have it (as fate would always have it), during a meditative hike along the river the next day we saw our crate of food. It was resting quietly at the base of a tree on a small island—upright and still intact. Apparently, our adventurous provisions could not resist the temptation to ride the rapids and were currently awaiting rescue in a stretch of the river that was conveniently, for the purposes of our retrieval efforts, not raging.

*****

In a sense, Theresa, Raylea, Sola, and I were all runaways. For different reasons and at different times in our lives we had left the worlds we had known, thrown caution to the wind, and slipped quietly into the unforeseeable.

The two young people who joined our mountain camping area that day were runaways in the traditional sense. They were each sixteen years old and had run away from the kind of homelives that imbued their eyes with a sadness that we recognized and empathized with instantly.

One of the things Theresa and I had in common was the fact that we were well-loved. Our parents loved us. Being loved unconditionally was something that we knew from birth. It's the kind of thing you can learn to see in people. The eyes of a person who grew up without love can't conceal that fact from someone who knows what to look for.

This boyfriend and girlfriend—babies in so many ways—had fled their homes for a life that, to us veterans of the road, they seemed profoundly unprepared to navigate. We were seeking. They were escaping. They had no plan beyond getting away from what we could only assume were hellish situations.

We were six years older than them but in worldliness we were old enough to be their parents. Under the watchful eyes of the two matriarchs who had done the same for us, we adopted them and wrapped them in the warm arms of our impromptu family of kindred spirits.

They looked so lost. We all ached for them.

I don't know what happened to these kids after we parted ways. I hope the world was good to them and that they grew to break the chains of neglect and abuse that life had dealt them.

I do know what happened to them while we were together.

The four of us took a walk in the woods. A short distance from where our provisions had once been briefly tethered there was a fallen tree bridging the river. Me and the boyfriend crossed without incident. The girlfriend slid off the tree and plunged into the river's merciless cascade. In an instant she was in a fight for her life against an opponent with unlimited and unrelenting power. She was hanging on to the fallen tree for dear life. The river was pounding her. It was entirely too much force for her to pull herself out and there was no footing within reaching distance for any of us to try to extract her. She was horizontal. The force of the water had already begun the process of pulling her body downriver. Only her face was above the water and the waves were covering it every two seconds. She was turning white. The water was freshly melted snow. It was freezing. She was freezing.

This happened over forty years ago. But right now my heart is racing and my hands are trembling above the keyboard. This is when I learned how, in a split second, a situation can change from one that is carefree to one where the most likely outcome is death.

A couple of paragraphs ago I said that Theresa and I felt like we could be these kid's parents. I was wrong about that. We were not nearly grown up enough to know how to deal with what was happening.

The boyfriend and I climbed into the water at the edge where the force wasn't overpowering. We each grabbed an overhanging branch with one hand to keep partially anchored to land. It looked to me that the river would push her toward us if she let go. But seriously, I had no idea what would happen.

Theresa was lying on the fallen tree. Their faces were inches from each other. Theresa kept screaming, "YOU ARE NOT GOING TO DROWN! Let go! Let go! They'll catch you!" The panic in this poor child's eyes was a sight neither of us will ever forget. She knew that these may be her last breaths in this world.

Finally, Theresa pulled her fingers from the death grip they held on the fallen tree and her body came hurtling down the rapids. If we had to step out more than a foot or two to get her all three of us would have gone downriver to certain, and I mean certain, death. In less than a second, she was as near to us as she would ever be and I and the sixteen-year-old runaway boyfriend with the sad eyes and the broken spirit reached out our free hands. Mine grabbed her shirt (which thankfully did not tear or pull off) and he snatched her arm. We pulled her, with more strength than either of us knew we could generate, out of the rampaging water and back into a life that really didn't need more trauma.

Water—Story Two

I am writing today at a cottage in the White Mountains of New Hampshire. The drinking water here comes from a well. There is no reason to believe that it isn't pure and safe.

I won't drink it. Not a single drop. I won't even put it on my toothbrush.

We had stayed with some friends in the mountains outside of Albuquerque for a while. It was there that Theresa and I picked up an intestinal parasite from the well water.

It took a few weeks to realize what had happened. But in time we came to the disconcerting realization that our bodies were supplying shelter and nutrition to a voracious microbe that was altogether unconcerned with the health of its hosts.

I don't need to go into detail about what it was like to be doing battle with dysentery while we were hitchhiking, standing in the rain, and sleeping on the ground. It's gross and you can just use your imagination.

I'm including the story because the resolution of the issue is a significant turning point in the tale of who we were and who we would become.

We would feel good for a few days and then become violently ill and then feel good again. Throughout the process we kept losing the one thing that, unlike today, we could not afford to lose: weight.

During this period of our youth, within the confines of certain arenas, Theresa and I were wiser than our years. Outside of those confines our level of wisdom and our common sense were often lower than one might expect from a bag of hammers.

We had just been part of the most remarkable gathering of alternative thinking that we had ever encountered. So naturally, we took the advice of a self-proclaimed medicine woman and were treating our dysentery problem with, and I kid you not, cayenne pepper and goldenseal root. Surprisingly to us (and to no one else) it didn't work. And we kept getting thinner and sicker and dumber.

Theresa had a pair of size 29 pants. Toward the end of this unfortunate ordeal, she was tying two belt loops together on each hip, effectively taking the waistline in three inches. I did the same on my size 30 jeans.

Finally, a woman we were camping with assessed our situation and made the statement that saved our lives. "You two are going to die. Go to the doctor!"

"Hmmm ... the doctor. Like a real whitecoat, Western medicine, kind of guy? Hadn't thought of that. But okay. We're always willing to try new things."

We went to a free clinic. The doctor put us on some good, old-fashioned, non-alternative, direct-to-the-point, no-fucking-around, drugs. And in one week we were not dead and were able to hold nourishment within our bodies again.

When our health returned, so did a modicum of our mutual common sense.

*****

Youth is an ambiguity-free zone. Young people always know what is right and what is wrong, what is good and what is bad, what sucks and what is awesome. Modern medicine: bad. Alternative medicine: awesome. North shore of Boston: Yuck. North shore of San Francisco: Yum. Simple. Clear. Unequivocable.

In the aftermath of having unwittingly assisted simple, clear, and unequivocable stupidity in its efforts to kill us, a moment of reflection seemed ineludible.

As the teller of this tale, I am now charged with the following tasks.

Find the best words in the English language to describe the moment when we began to realize that we had crossed the outer edge of how much hippie philosophy and practices we could continue to embrace. And how that moment started our gradual movement back in the direction of the practical, earthbound worldview from which we had skedaddled.

But I don't want to. I'm burned out. I've been typing for nine hours. I am presently suffering from an acute, and possibly terminal, case of synonym fatigue. If my thesaurus was a man, I would use a hundred one-syllable words to tell him that he's a pompous ass. I do not want to unearth one more word that my friends will have to dust off their dictionaries to understand. So, I'm giving the job to Mickey the line crew foreman.

Take it away Mick.

Hey Kid,

To me it's simple. You left heah thinkin' ya friends were all idiots and that those guys doing the meditatin', what did you call them ... kunda-weenies? That those dudes were smaht. Well, maybe you and all the weirdos you met after you left heah ahh friggin' geniuses. But theah ain't a guy on this crew or a daytime bahtendah in this town or a toothless hockey playah in the entiah world dumb enough to think you can cuah dysentery with cayenne peppah.

Look, some of your friends ahh idiots. And some hippies ahh smaht. With the exceptions of Irish whiskey and syphilis, nothin' is all good or all bad in this world. Your job is to learn everything and then decide what to keep and what to chuck out the windah. It's all about choices. Did you know that I had a full scholahship to Wentworth Institute of Technology? I coulda got an engineerin' degree, but I chose to take the job with the city and be a well-paid, full-time drunk instead.

Choices.

You and ya girl ain't gonna end up bein' one hundred percent palookas from Lynn and ya ain't gonna be full-time meditatin' weirdos eithah. The sweet spot is in the middle and you need to make good choices on what weirdo shit is worth keepin' and what ain't. (I'm suggestin' that takin' cayenne out of the medicine cabinet and puttin' it back on the spice rack might be a good place to staht.)

Look, you've been gone long enough. You don't need to keep lumpin' everything and everybody in this town into an all-negative category anymoah. Some of the freaks you met and some of the stuff you did in your travels look pretty interestin' to me. (I'd like to get me one of them group massages some day.) But a lot of it is just bullshit and a waste of time. And a lot of the stuff you were raised with has real-world value and shouldn't be thrown out with the bathwatah.

If we eliminate the people heah who fit the stereotype—you know, the guys fightin' ovah the girl and the kids pukin' ovah the fence. What's left ahh the people who drag theiah asses out of bed and go to work every day. People who know the value of hahd work and how to stretch a dollah. Guys who will loan you theiah last twenty bucks because they know that feelin' of havin' empty pockets. Let me ask you this. When ya watah heatah bursts will you be callin' a lucid dreamah to fix it? No. You'll call me—not after 2:00 in the afternoon cause I'll be lit—but in the maughnin'. I'll drop what I'm doin' and come and fix ya plumbin'. And I won't take any money because I know ya broke and I know how bein' broke feels. Theah's a lot heah that can go into the trashcan. But it's time to drop the attitude and salvage some of the things we have heah that will come in real handy in a world that doesn't give a shit about how well-read you ahh.

This story is slowly turnin' you back toward the real world—

you know the one wheah everyone isn't thinkin' about peace and love—wheah some of them are tryna hustle ya outta ya money.

You know, every time I saw ya mothah, she told me to go fry my ass. One time I heard ya fathah tell a loudmouth, bullshit aahtist at Kenny's Bah that he was as soft as a sneakah full of shit. This attitude and these ways to express it took yeahs to develop. Don't underestimate theiah real-world value.

When no one is tryin' ta hustle ya, you can meditate and space out and read philosophy till the friggin' cows come home. But when they ahh, ya gonna need all ya Lynn skills to keep from getting' ya ass handed to you by this world.

Good luck kid.

Hope this helps.

Onward

When the joyous, exhilarating, spiritually and intellectually nourishing activities at Camp Cosmic were at their high water mark we thought, "Wouldn't it be great if life could always be like this."

It wouldn't.

We knew that now. Places and groups and moments in time like that exist for accelerated growth spurts and emotional/spiritual battery recharging. That's how I say it now. Back then I would have said it like this: "Once your batteries are fully charged, it's time to stop pointing your flashlight at the sun man."

We stood in the campground with our backpacks strapped to our shoulders and secured around our waists. My guitar was in my hand. Lijah was beside us in full road-dog regalia. It was time to go—time to take the new version of who we were back on the road. Raylee and Sola sat beside each other in folding chairs next to their van. They waved goodbye and told us that we were beautiful. Minutes later the highway would sweep us away from them and the vestiges of the community we had all created. It felt like leaving home.

We spent the summer in the Rocky Mountains where cooler temperatures made outdoor living easier. We went back to Colorado. But instead of returning to Boulder we visited Aspen and Vail.

There was a girl in our high school who was so movie-star beautiful that she looked like she had been manufactured by a modeling agency. Aspen and Vail made me think of her. I suspected that in their quiet moments these towns wished they had been born ugly or just moderately beautiful. They are both encircled by the kind of spectacular panoramic mountain vistas that attract the Lamborghini people whose wealth can buy them whatever they want. And what they want is to have, and be seen with, the most beautiful of all woman.

Vagabonding was uncomfortable there. We left after a week to visit a series of other mountain communities where not being a millionaire didn't draw attention and the residents had a less myopic view of beauty.

We had been much less frugal with our money on this adventure and it was running out. Our plan was to pick fruit in Washington State in the fall and go to Guatemala in the winter.

Why Guatemala?

Someone had told us it was awesome.

What about the dog and the no passport thing?

Huh? We'll deal with that stuff at the border. It'll work out.

On our way up the coast of Oregon and Washington in September we noticed what appeared to us to be groups of Grateful Dead fans walking slowly through fields on the side of the roads as if they were looking for a lost contact lens. "What are they doing?" I asked a driver." "Shroom hunting," he replied.

Ahh, the Pacific Northwest, where every autumn families gather to enjoy the great outdoors and partake in the ancient tradition of foraging for psychedelic psilocybin mushrooms.

We picked D'Angelo pears for five weeks that fall in Washington. The people we worked alongside were a curious and compelling mix of transients. There were some hitchhiking wanderers like us. But unlike us, a lot of these folks were members of the permanently unleashed—picking fruit in the fall, planting trees in the winter and enjoying freedom in a warm location of their choosing for the rest of the year. Home for them was in the center of the freedom that seasonal work and constant movement provided.

Several of our fellow pickers were members of the Hoedads— a remarkable egalitarian, worker-owned cooperative whose full title is the Hoedads Reforestation Cooperative. It started in 1970 and ran till 1994. They would bid on government contracts and became very successful by delivering groups of workers who excelled at the art of tree planting using an all-for-one-and-one-for-all team method. They were the first to hire women as tree planters. A full twenty-five percent of the force were women. These were not flower children. They were tough and organized and impressive. You should read about them. (I know, technically you are reading about them now. But google them. I'll wait.)

Boy Dogs

Years ago, being a conscientious pet owner, I had my male dog neutered. On the ride home I couldn't bring myself to look at him. No dissertations on the long-term benefits of neutering were going to alter his understanding of, and his feelings about, what had just happened. I knew what he was thinking: "Look me in the eye you bastard! You Claudius! You Iago! A plague upon your house you most treacherous villain! When you were drunk and lying on the floor and no one in the family was talking to you, who showed you unconditional love? And *this* is how you repay my loyalty? I keep going down to lick my junk and guess what? No junk. Where is my junk?"

Today, an unleashed, unneutered dog on the street would show up on your Facebook feed under the title "Photo of unleashed dog with testicles goes viral." In the seventies they were everywhere.

All the fruit tramps, which is what we pickers were affectionately called, had dogs. Lijah was the only female. She chose this extraordinarily inopportune time to go into her first heat.

The word spread quickly among the dogs in the orchard that Lijah was in the market for a suitor. I looked down from the top of a ladder and saw a motley, fully-testicled, assemblage of wannabe canine fathers encircling our dog who was leashed to the base of a pear tree. Since none of these unprincipled indigents bothered to show me the courtesy of asking my permission for her hand, I considered them all unworthy of even the slightest consideration.

Everything you will ever need to know about the boundless, unrestrainable power of libido can be seen in the crazed eyes of a pack of unneutered male dogs who have picked up the scent of an ovulating female. There is just no reasoning with them. No amount of pleading or explaining about the future ramifications of their actions, no questions about who is going to support these puppies, no barricades, no yelling of obscenities, and no number of pears bounced off their noggins, will divert their laser-focused attention from the job at hand.

That evening our shack was besieged by a horde of incurably infatuated boy dogs. They encircled our humble dwelling and subjected us to a chorus of lovesick whining and howling, and the occasional reciting of a sonnet. (I may have dreamed that last one.)

In the morning we implemented the plan we had devised while under siege. We took a pair of my underwear (briefs, not boxers), pulled them over Lijah's two rear legs and then slid her tail through the little pee hole that no one ever uses. That final maneuver kept the underwear from falling down. It looked like a diaper, but it was actually an inspired piece of improvisational contraceptive ingenuity.

The next day our corner of the orchard was transformed into a surrealist dreamscape that featured all manner of male dog wooing techniques and canine pugilism. Several of Lijah's potential beaus engaged in what to me seemed like a fantastical display of bipedal animated cartoon fisticuffs that day. Periodically, a victorious alpha male would approach the object of his desire to collect his hard-won reward only to be denied the ultimate satisfaction by Lijah's low-budget, homemade chastity belt. We were pleased. Lijah was not. I don't think she ever completely forgave us.

Stop Drop

Beneath the shack the orchard owner had provided us, we discovered years' worth of half-used, rusting cannisters of pesticides.

I learned many things from my time in the orchards. What has best stood the test of time is my understanding of how many questionable chemicals have been sprayed on that commercially grown apple you are feeding your child.

That unfortunate piece of produce was baptized with pesticides when it was just a wee bud and never saw a sustained period of not being sprayed with poison until it was shipped to the supermarket.

The last (and some say the greatest) of the many chemicals sprayed on a pre-picked piece of fruit in the nineteen seventies was Daminozide, known at the time by its trade name Alar and by fruit pickers as Stop Drop.

This marvel of modern agriculture is a plant growth regulator—a chemical sprayed on fruit to regulate growth, make harvest easier, and keep apples from falling off the trees before they ripen so they are red and firm for storage and shipment.

"Here you go little Timmy. An apple a day. Yum."

The orchard where we were working on that warm October afternoon was separated from another farmer's property by a dirt road. We were working the trees that were near the road. Imagine our surprise when we heard a plane engine and looked up to see that the neighbor was crop dusting his apples with Stop Drop. We were all summarily covered with Daminozide.

This chemical was removed from use by the EPA in 1989. It was never, to my knowledge, removed from the internal organs of any pear pickers who were dusted with it that day.

I don't know how to explain how I felt when we were leaving the orchard after being aerially poisoned and treated with the same consideration one might give to an infestation of cockroaches. But it sure as hell left an impression on me. I think about it when I hear people criticizing migrant workers. I think about it every time I am in the grocery store. I think about it every time I see a kid eating an apple or a pear. I thought about it when we lived in Maine across the street from a blueberry farm in the nineteen eighties. I was standing beside my pregnant wife and holding my one year old's hand when a crop duster flew low over our house and dumped the pesticide Guthion (a neurotoxin derived from nerve agents developed during World War II) directly across the street. I think about it whenever I have reason to ponder how the well-being of employees is valued by their employers.

Change

After several months in the womb, I was loving my world. It was just warm enough, just wet enough, there was a cord that brought me a steady stream of food, and there were friendly voices saying sweet and loving things to me through the wall. I had learned everything I needed to know about my environment. Life was good. I said, "This place is perfect. I could stay here forever."

One second later the same walls that had protected me from the outside world began to turn against me. They squeezed me tight in a very unloving manner and then stopped. At first, I was like "Whoa, that was cool." But when it happened again, I was like, "Whoa, this ain't cool no more. What's happening? Am I moving? I don't want to move. Where am I going? I love it here. Everything is perfect. I don't want to leave. Who's gonna feed me? What's that light at the end of the tunnel? I need to talk to the manager. This is unacceptable."

Then I was forced against my will down a long tunnel and pushed out into a horrifying new world. Everything I knew and loved was gone. I was cold. I had to figure out how to breathe. And it was WAY TOO BRIGHT! I cried and cried and cried because I was terrified of change and I wanted to go back to where everything was familiar and I didn't have to learn anything new.

Eventually I got used to my new world. The light wasn't so bad. These huge people wrapped me up in blankets when I got cold and even though I missed the cord that would bring my food, I grew quite fond of these awesome round things that I could suck milk out of. "Okay, I can live with this." Five years later, it wasn't just okay, it was great. There were toys to play with and cool stuff to learn every day. The two big people were awesome. They were always nearby and came running whenever I needed them. They made me feel safe and loved. I thought, "I could stay here forever."

And then ...

"Wait, what do you mean, 'I'm five now and I have to go to school on that bus by myself?' This is a joke, right? You guys are messing with me, right? Good one. No? You're serious? This cannot be happening to me. I am going to cry and cry and cry until you let me stay home."

Change, whether I am prepared for it or not, is the one constant in my life.

*****

With our pockets overflowing with fruit-picking money, we wandered southward. Guatemala, here we come. All the way down the coasts of Washington, Oregon and Northern California Ms. Theresa wasn't feeling well. Probably a cold or some residual effects from your run-of-the-mill, aerial, chemical poisoning we thought. Nope. She was pregnant.

I must say that I have become quite fond of these moments where the world I have spent years creating leaves a note on the bureau that reads. "I love you. It's been great. But I need to move on. Believe me, in time you'll see that this is best for both of us." No talking it over. No long discussions on how to make the transition less abrupt. I just wake up one day to learn that the life I've been living called a cab while I was sleeping, kissed me on the forehead and slipped away. My appreciation comes from knowing that without these periodic abandonments, I would stagnate within the walls of the comfortable and the familiar.

It's as if every new chapter of my life has a built-in fail-safe trigger that ignites and blows everything up when there is nothing more to learn and I am in danger of becoming the equivalent of the old guy at the office who refuses to learn how to use the computer.

There is something beautiful about gathering up the remains of a blown-up life's lessons in the hope that some of them might prove useful in whatever new life is coming.

After we rejected the idea of trying to squeeze in a Central American journey before her third trimester, Theresa and I slowly began to contemplate parenthood. We spent early winter at our home bases in California, Arizona, and New Mexico saying long slow goodbyes to our friends and to the life we had embraced for so long.

Somewhere in Southern California we had been dropped off at night on a ramp. We looked around in the dark and decided that the patch of bushes nearby was sufficiently secluded. Then we laid down to sleep once more beneath the stars. We talked for half the night about how we were going to take the job of raising this child seriously. I always knew that Theresa would be a great mom. But I also felt that I would be good at the dad thing. I was willing to work at a crappy job and do whatever else was necessary to survive. And I could picture myself being perfectly at home with a kid on my knee. It was obvious to us that we were going to be excellent parents.

When we woke up that morning, we realized that we had not been sleeping in a secluded area. Because every passing car, everyone filling up at the gas station across the street, and all the people having breakfast at the diner were staring at us.

Under the watchful and bemused eyes of all these Californians, while fully illuminated by the morning sunlight, we arose and rolled up our sleeping bags. While I was brushing my teeth and spitting tooth paste onto the ground with my hair pointing in multiple directions, Theresa was bent over at the waist with a bout of morning sickness. I waved and smiled at the window-seated diner patrons and thought, "their opinion of our child-rearing potential is probably a teensy bit less flattering than the one we have for ourselves."

In December our parents bought us each a plane ticket and we flew from Albuquerque to Boston. That was it. The memory box that held these road stories was closed and locked and tucked away for over forty years in the closet of two people who were raising a family.

Two Vagabonds in Disguise

Our post-vagabond, soon-to-be-parents era began in a cottage at Stickney's Corner in Washington, Maine that had been empty for years and was rented to us for seventy-five dollars a month. It had no running water and a two-seater outhouse that was located in a small barn connected to the house.

We thought it was heaven. My parents felt differently. "Look Dad, there are two seats so you and Ma can hold hands while you're pooping. What could be more romantic than that?"

"Don't be a smartass. Let's take a ride." We drove up a mountain road. He parked the car at a scenic overview. The evening birds were singing. The sun was setting. The horizon was ablaze in pink and purple. The mountains in the distance were snow-capped and majestic. It was a scene that was begging to be immortalized by the skillful hand of an artist.

After a few minutes in quiet appreciation, my dad asked, "What the fuck are you doing up here?" I laughed so hard it took a few minutes for me to gain my composure and say, "I'm trying to get back to the earth Dad." To which he replied, "I don't know what that means but if it means being dirt poor the rest of your life, then you're doing a hell of a job son." He slid me a twenty-dollar bill and said, "Don't tell your mother I gave you this. I'm glad you're back."

*****

The locals called us flatlanders. It is not a term of endearment. Eventually I came to understand the full meaning of the word. But there isn't a way to translate it to non-Mainers that accurately expresses the multilayered levels of contempt that it so succinctly communicates to those who are fluent in the local dialect. Remembering that any translation of this term can only express twenty percent of its full meaning, this is the best I can offer: You ain't from here. You ain't ever going to be from here. Go back to your godawful state.

At first we thought they hated us. And maybe they did, but eventually we grew to realize that we were providing them something to gossip about and a much-needed source of entertainment. "All right, who's got January fifteenth in the pool for the date those two hippies freeze to death in that house?"

The man who lived across the street was flawlessly created to embody the stereotype of an ornery old Mainer. He lived alone. No one ever wondered why. He was merciless with the flatlander taunts. But he was also helpful, kind, and generous to us while never letting us forget that we weren't welcome in his state. It was weird, but not that uncommon. People we met in parts of Idaho were like that. They helped us, fed us, and showed us kindness while letting us know that they didn't like us or our lifestyle.

This guy ran a hose from his house through the culvert under the street to our kitchen so we could have running water when the temperature was above freezing.

We were in his kitchen one day thanking him for that kind and neighborly gesture. After our show of gratitude I said, "Our baby is going to be born in that house across the street. You can say whatever you want about us being flatlanders, but this kid is going to be a Mainer." And then, with the perfect timing of a sly old Maine Yankee, he paused, looked me in the eye and said, "Well, if your cat climbs in the oven to have kittens, you don't call them biscuits now do ya?"

*****

It was February. The guy who took the January fifteenth date had lost the pool. We didn't freeze. We were in fact, quite toasty in our little cottage with our wood stove blazing and our new life unfolding and becoming clearer each day.

Theresa was sitting in an old rocking chair that someone's grandmother had given us. I was seated on a well-worn couch that entered our world under similar circumstances.

We were drinking herbal tea. I was thinking that a cup of chamomile on a Friday night presented a compelling argument to support the theory that those two party animals who left Lynn, Massachusetts five years earlier were either gone or incognito.

The sun had just gone down. The twilight warmed the room with a delicate amber hue. Theresa was looking out the window. There were wisps of steam rising from the cup in her hand. The soft natural light on her face and the way it lit the room made her look like a master painter's portrait from the seventeen-hundreds. I see this image in my mind today as if it is framed in a gallery.

I had loved this dark-haired beauty from the minute I laid eyes on her. And with each shared experience my love for her has grown deeper.

I recall looking at her that evening and becoming helplessly awash in emotion. It was too much to process—all our implausible history together—how alone we felt in our home community. How much we each hungered for art and literature and deeper thinking and to experience the infinite possibilities that we instinctively knew were out there beyond the city limits. How we both found the one other person who felt equally out of place and was willing to step into the unknown and not look back. How she loved me and believed that I could become the person I hoped I could be. How she helped me dare to dream.

I had never experienced deeper love for anyone or anything than I did while gazing upon her living portrait that day.

In the first chapter of this story, I said that my old man's eyes still saw this woman as nineteen years old in a summer dress hitchhiking beside me in the desert. That is the image I have of her when I'm feeling happy or playful or naughty.

This image—this masterpiece—comes to me in much more serious moments. It is the picture I see when I think that … when I think that … I may outlive her.

*****

The portrait moved and broke the spell.

Theresa turned to me and said, "I believe that at this moment in time we are literally penniless. There's no bank account, no food stamps, no job, and not one single penny in this house."

I asked, "Should we panic?"

She said, "I believe we should. I think it's what normal people would do in this situation."

I said, "Right. Normal people would be flipping out right now. I mean, we're living in a real house and we're going to have a real baby—hell, someone might even give us a real television set. We're definitely on our way to becoming normal. So we should freak all the way out and not have any faith that things will work out or that the universe loves us or any of that stuff that the Normals think is hippie nonsense and a waste of time."

She said, "Yup, we need to learn how to make the worst of every situation at the earliest point so we can be freaking out every day like everyone else. It's going to take some practice."

I said, "Okay, do you want to start? How about you scream at me and tell me that I need to get up off my ass and go get a job?"

She said, "That's a good one. And then you can storm out and go to the bar. You won't have any money but when you tell the bartender what a shrew your wife is, he'll let you open a tab."

I said, "None of this sounds too hard. I don't think we're going to have any trouble learning to behave in a way that makes every situation ten times worse than it really is. And, since I am fully committed to becoming normal with you my dear, I'm happy to practice these tiresome lines and unevolved behaviors. But first, let's try to disprove your penniless theory. I still think there may be a coin or two hidden in this house somewhere."

Theresa opened the living room closet and slid her hand into all the jacket pockets. There were no pennies. I pulled the cushions off the couch. I pushed my hand down in the sides where the coinage that slides out of trouser pockets hides. I locked eyes with Theresa. A smile came across my face. She returned my smile with a look of excitement. I said, "I think this is it. I think we have avoided pennilessness my darling." Then I slowly pulled my hand out and revealed to our eternal dismay that no, it was just a nickel-size piece of hard candy.

We had just confirmed that at this moment in our long, extraordinarily atypical journey we were indeed without one solitary cent. In addition, we were unemployed, lacking most skill sets that might alter that fact, expecting a baby, hauling water in buckets, and going out to a barn in subzero temperatures to pee.

It was perfect.

The love of my life and I gazed into each other's eyes with sly grins on our faces. We had a full understanding of the challenges of the moment—they were plentiful and powerful. And I imagine that to many couples they would seem insurmountable. But they were simply no match for what we had experienced on the road. From the bottom to the top of the continent, over a three-year period, we lived, traveled, and grew into entirely new people, on faith and the kindness of strangers. Sure, there was a baby in the mix now—but think about it, we weren't all alone and thousands of miles from our support system any more. All our relatives and friends lived close by and were anxious to help us. Comparatively, this was going to be a piece of cake. I was expecting my mind to produce an encapsulation of all the unlikely circumstances and events that conspired to create this moment. I imagined it would be delivered in a concise manner that I could archive and retrieve later—perhaps to help pull this story together in these final pages. But I just kept thinking about the last scene in the movie *Zorba the Greek*.

Everything that Zorba and Basil built together had just crashed into the sea. The future they had planned together was snatched away in an instant. After a few moments of coming to terms with their sudden new reality, Zorba says to Basil "You have everything but one thing: madness. A man needs a little madness or else he never dares cut the rope and be free." Then after a thoughtful pause Basil asks Zorba to teach him to dance. The movie ends with them dancing on the beach.

I said to Theresa, "Milady, we have not a single penny and circumstances have placed such fortified battalions of misfortune before us that we shall certainly not live to see the morning. I believe that there is only thing that can be done."

I bent one knee halfway to the floor, reached forward my hand and said, "May I have the honor of this dance?" After some coy exaggerated hesitation, she acquiesced, took my hand, and rose regally from her chair.

I placed my right hand upon her side and held her right hand with my left. And with our unborn child pressed snugly between us, we waltzed to the music that plays only in the hearts of two vagabonds in disguise.

THE ARDUOUS JOURNEY OF MARIA'S SMILE

The Scituate Smile

Is it legal to live in Scituate, Massachusetts and not be blonde? That is the question in my mind that is responsible for this wry grin on my face as I sit in a café placed strategically inside this upscale mall alongside Route 3A while blonde after blonde after blonde orders slightly overpriced low-fat muffins and lattes.

I am in a wealthy town on Boston's south shore and lots of white people live here, that part I get. But the rules on what qualifies as being white here seem to have been distilled down to an interpretation that excludes even people of Mediterranean extraction. On the rare occasions when I have seen someone here who appears to be Greek, Italian, or Portuguese, I can't help but assume that they are either working here for a Nordic family or, like me, are just stopping by to bask in the overabundance of yellow as they pass through this enclave into America.

For twenty years now I have installed security systems in homes in this part of the state. As easy as it would be for a

grizzled old factory-town proletarian like me to mock and mimic
these folks, the truth is that they are often very nice people who,
in their own way of course, sincerely want the world to be a
better place for those less fortunate than themselves.

Many of the people I have worked for here are active in
organizations that give invaluable support to human beings in the
United States and abroad who very likely could not survive
without such support. The fact that the recipients of this benevolence would have to hit the lottery and dye their hair to feel
comfortable living in the community from which this sustenance
is dispensed is interesting in a quizzical sort of way but is not
germane to the telling of this story.

*****

I'm guessing that she is in her mid-twenties as I watch her enter
the café from the mall. She is carrying something bulky, perhaps
a pair of shoes, in a bag with a strong string handle. She is
wearing, I surmise, four hundred and fifty dollars' worth of
clothing, footwear, and accessories. Not a big deal here, it doesn't
make her stand out. In fact she seems to have hit the exact center
of the price range for an ensemble that a woman would wear on
a casual hour of shoe shopping at the mall in this town.

Her face is lovely with smooth skin and bright blue eyes that
are nicely enhanced with just the right amount of makeup. The
girl at the counter is obviously her friend. When she slides a
double latte across the counter while saying something funny a
smile pops out of the young shopper's face as if it had been resting
there all morning behind her teeth. It is fresh and energetic. It
exposes forty grand worth of dental work on teeth so white they
hurt my eyes. Then it slips back behind her lips to await the next
clever but innocuous quip from another thin blonde girl she went
to high school with in this lovely, lovely town.

Bird Man—Part One

The living room of Joseph Collins's home in coastal Maine is essentially a photo gallery of the world's most spectacular birds. Having spent the bulk of his youth traversing the earth's most remote mountains and jungles patiently seeking out and then photographing all the most breathtakingly colorful feathered creatures known to man he is widely considered, among those who make it their business to consider such things, to have done it better than anyone else.

Interspersed between award-winning in-flight framed color photographs of such explosively plumaged winged things as the Resplendent Quetzal and the Hyacinth Macaw are plaques from almost every Audubon society and international photography group in the world, all proclaiming his greatness in subtle variations of the same twenty words.

The walls of his house are a permanent shrine to the time in Joseph's life when he believed that the beautiful and the spectacular were inseparable and incapable of existing without one another.

Maria's Smile—Part One

"Where can I get a cup of coffee at this hour of night?" "If you don't want to drive out to Route 9 you can walk to the Colombian donut shop. It's dirty and the coffee is dreadful but it's close." A bit shy of a ringing endorsement but I was, I admit, intrigued.

I sit on a stool at the counter and try to guess the waitress's age. It's hopeless. Her face is weathered. Her eyes have such a deep sadness, which I assume has been created in equal parts by poverty, bad luck, bad decisions, and God only knows what else—that she could be anywhere from forty to sixty years old.

This is a face that has been sculpted by a life full of struggle, survival, and interestingness.

She hypnotizes me.

While she stands before me assuming that I might eventually open my mouth and order something, I am wondering just what it would take for me—a fifth-generation white American male—to get her to open up and give me the half a day it would take to tell me her story.

I awake from this delusion, sense her impatience, and order a small coffee with cream.

The sleeve of my shirt is sticking to something that was spilled on the counter earlier today. (I'm being generous here. It may have been last week for all I know.) As I sip my coffee and note silently that it is indeed dreadful, I turn away from the counter and try to hide the grin that has just appeared on my face from the thought of how dedicated I am to my work that I routinely fight the bacteria and poison coffee of these trenches in proud pursuit of the world's most interesting stories.

She observes that I am grinning for no apparent reason and becomes even more cautious and wary. At this moment I decide that I need to see her smile. I become so curious (obsessed really) about what it will take to get her to smile and what a smile on the lips of a face so hardened will look like that I decide with my usual obliviousness to the social, ethnic, and racial realities of the situation to try to charm her.

I ask her what her name is. I say a few things that I think are charming. I'm working it hard—charm, charm, flirt, flirt, charm, charm, flirt ... nothing. Well, not exactly nothing. Some disdain and mild contempt for sure.

As a last resort I thank her for what I say is truly the greatest cup of coffee I have ever had the pleasure of drinking. And then I see it—as subtle a hint of acknowledgement that a face this weathered can reveal. It isn't even a flinch. A flinch would have been dramatic in comparison. It is an infinitesimal lightening of her eyes. I bet there aren't ten people in the world who would have noticed it. I feel like a champion poker player who just picked up a "tell" from another champion player.

What I had just described as the greatest cup of coffee on earth probably killed the last person who drank one. It was funny. She knew it and I knew she was going to smile. But I would need to be patient if I wanted to witness it because what was eventually to turn up the corners of Maria's mouth was not a smile that had been resting comfortably behind forty grand of dental work all day. It was something entirely different.

Bird Man—Part Two

The leaves on the ground in his yard were moving. He could see it through the window in his living room. Slowly opening the back door and crouching down he saw that it was, as he had hoped, a white-throated sparrow—a bird so common (millions of them in North America) and so plain that it is often listed by birders, when it is noticed at all, as one of the "little brown birds."

Weighing approximately one ounce, this bird, during migration, flies long distances at night without stopping to rest at an altitude so high that it is virtually invisible and therefore safe from the ever-present possibility of becoming a midnight snack for an owl or other predator.

"Drawn helplessly to color and light a man's eyes are a traitor to real beauty," he thought; as he slowly went outside to admire this tiny visitor with the nondescript attire and the amazing life story.

"What must it be like to be so small and fly so high for thousands of miles all the while knowing that during the flight you will burn off every calorie you had consumed in the preceding days and that you will be so near death when you finally land that if there is no food readily available you will surely expire? What is it in the makeup of a living thing that causes it to cast reason aside and hurl itself into a migration of uncertainty where death from exhaustion is as likely an outcome as survival?"

"Who could know how many are lost and what moments of terror take place on your thousand-mile journey through unforgiving night sky?"

"You are so common and so plain my friend, but these are not the eyes of a child that find beauty in only those things that shine gazing in wonderment upon you today. These are the eyes of a man who has seen many long winters, lost many a dear one, and learned many hard lessons about love and beauty. And I dare say that you have chanced upon the one garden in Maine where the gardener has lived long enough to know that true beauty is seen through the deeper eyes of knowledge. It is your heart and the challenges it has enabled you to overcome with such quiet grace that makes you and your song so profoundly beautiful."

Maria's Smile—Part Two

From a base camp in her solar plexus Maria's smile begins its nearly impossible journey toward her lips. Unlike the smiles of many suburban American women, Maria's must run the gauntlet of her life's memories. But, not unlike the Atlantic salmon that is surely unaware of the myriad of obstacles it must overcome on its journey upstream to spawn, when the time is right the genetic makeup of Maria's smile requires it to lunge headfirst toward her lips with no thought about all the damnable remembrances lying in wait at every turn to pummel the naïveté out of the Little Smile That Could.

I count exactly one minute and thirty seconds from the conception of the smile revealed to me in the lightening of her eyes until its fleeting appearance upon her face. In that time I watch as it is attacked by hundreds of memories, each one beating it about the head and shoulders with some painful recollection from her solitary journey from complete anonymity in the ghettos of Bogotá to complete anonymity in this urban American coffee shop.

Poverty, hunger, humiliation, soldiers, violence, bodies, more bodies, border guards, thirsty babies, hungry babies, dying babies.

What was left of Maria's smile after running the memory gauntlet of her life was a weary sojourner barely alive and silently proclaiming the invincibility of the human spirit.

Using the morsel of strength it had managed to retain, it pushed up the corners of Maria's mouth exactly one quarter of one inch for exactly three seconds and shined a light so indescribably resplendent upon this small corner of the world that it blessed everyone in the room with eyes wise enough to see and appreciate the depth and magnitude of its beauty. Then, like a little brown bird, it flitted away.

BEHIND THE WALL

1968: Don't Tell Me What to Do

In sixty-four years of living only a handful of people outside my family have ever raised their voice to me in anger. I'm always surprised when it happens. I still can't believe that anyone wouldn't know by looking at me that the part of my personality that alerts me to unreasonable authority, having been steeled in the white-hot furnace of my formative years, is a complex, manipulative, and ruthless opponent who will decipher and attack the weaknesses of any distributor of perceived injustice with calculated and obstinate tenacity.

I'm the oldest child—the one my parents experimented on. I fought all the battles. I learned to play the long game. I taught myself how to identify the weaknesses of those with power over me and to be patient and calculating when exploiting them. I assume that my younger siblings appreciate the fact that the reason they were raised by battle-weary fragments of the parents I knew is directly attributable to my youthful soldiering.

I feel obligated here to thank my children for not turning out like my parents' first-born son. I look back now in quiet horror at the cold-bloodedness that I brought into battle with my parents from age nine till I left home at seventeen.

In 1968 I was in the sixth grade and well down the road to turning bad. I was flunking all my subjects and probably going to be held back. I devised a plan with my friend to run away from home on the day we would receive our report cards. We stored supplies under my front porch. We planned to meet on our way home and sneak off before our parents got to see how bad we were doing in school.

I got my report card on a Friday—three Fs, two Ds and a C. As I was approaching our runaway stash I saw my mother walking toward me. Shit! The jig is up. She knows. I ran down the railroad tracks toward Saugus with her screaming behind me to stop. I had no jacket, no food, no money, no plan, no accomplice, and absolutely no fear. Being alone in the world did not scare me.

After the sun had gone down I recall walking down Route 1 singing the Vanilla Fudge version of the Supremes' song "Set Me Free Why Don't You Babe? Get outta My Life Why Don't You Babe?"

No fear.

The one thing, perhaps the only thing, I did fear was the curtailing of my personal freedom that would have begun that evening after Mom and Dad saw a report card that begged the question, "Do you do anything at all in school?" Then, like now, if you want to see the warrior in me, just use your power to threaten my freedom.

I walked two towns over to Malden. I was hungry and cold but not homesick or afraid; just the victim of poor planning and out of options. I walked into a Catholic church. Eventually a priest saw me. He sat down with me. I told him my story. He made me a peanut butter and jelly sandwich, called my parents, and drove me home.

Today my parents are both dead. I have grandchildren who are the same age that I was that evening as I walked along old Route 1 singing songs of freedom with no coat, no plan, and no clue. I have been stuck at the beginning of this next paragraph for six days. Each time I attempt to document this regrettable moment of my history I get crushed by the thought of what it would feel like to be sitting at home waiting for seven hours knowing only that my beautiful, clueless eleven-year-old is all alone at night in the great big scary world.

Crushed.

Incapacitated.

And unable to continue.

Empathy. The decades have filled me with it. It is the thing that, until now, has stood between me and the honest telling of this story.

The priest rang our doorbell. My mother opened the door. Cigarette smoke from seven hours of chain smoking was clouding the ceiling tiles as light from the big fluorescent bulb shone through. My parents looked like soldiers who had just escaped from a prisoner of war camp. They were relieved that the ordeal was over but were visibly and perhaps permanently damaged from the horror of the experience.

They thanked the priest. They told me to go to bed and that we would talk in the morning.

I felt nothing.

Actually, to be honest, even though the typing of this is dripping salt water onto my keyboard, I did feel something. I felt a sense of victory. No one was punishing me. No one was limiting my freedom. I got exactly what I wanted. The trail of terror and heartache that smoldered behind me in the hearts of my family, although devastating upon reflection, was of no concern to me then.

Breaking Up with My Muse

I think we need to see other people. Don't look at me like that. You know this has been coming for a long time. I always thought that this was a partnership. But it has never been that. It has always been about you. What *you* want. What *you* need. And what I can do to turn *your* wants and needs into something real.

How many countless, irretrievable hours, days, and weeks have I spent sequestered in a tiny room torturing myself over what exact words to use on some poem, song or story idea that you swore was brilliant only to find out later that it was stupid and not worth one minute of time?

And where did the time I used to polish these turds come from? Oh, I don't know, maybe from learning a trade? You know, without a lifetime of constant distractions I could have been a plumber. I could have made fifty bucks an hour and be nearing retirement with a full pension.

And let's not forget the alienation. You made me skip school at fifteen years old and sit in Lynn Woods reading *Siddhartha*. Why? You knew I had to live in this town with the sons and daughters of football-loving proletarians for whom the suspicion that I might possess even a modest vocabulary was all the justification needed to kick my artsy ass.

Remember the job I had paving driveways that summer in Maine with that crew of the newly unincarcerated? How long did it take them to figure out that I was a weirdo who wrote poetry? "Hey Shakespeare see that babe walking by? Why don't you write us a sonnet about how beautiful her ass is?"

I have suffered merciless harassment and alienation and have been surrounded and tortured by disproportionately empowered illiterates all my life and I'm sick of it.

I'm breaking up with you. Never call me again.

Apologizing to My Muse

I'm sorry. Please forgive me. I didn't really mean any of those things I said.

I wish I was on Ambien. Then I could say it was a bad reaction. But it appears that I do not need the support of pharmaceuticals to behave ungraciously. So I have no choice but to own it. I'll understand if you never speak to me again. But just hear me out.

The alienation that you filled my formative years with forced me to become an astute observer. Initially it was a survival skill that enabled me to predict and elude confrontations that might be coming my way. But later that attentiveness helped me to become a writer who could occasionally create work that resonated.

I suppose I could go on about our creative accomplishments and the fulfilling and interesting life we have created but all I have been able to think about today is the word "Home."

When I was a boy and my dad was whiskey drunk I would be awakened from the sweet dreams of youth by angry voices. There in the vulnerable half-conscious twilight between dream and day as I was freefalling toward the awakened world—and before I could don the armor my mind had created to shield my unhardened heart—I knew the terror of a rabbit being carried to the fox den.

At the moment before transitioning to the physical world I would feel that you—my inner voice, my trusted consigliere, my hiding place, my brilliant and tenacious enemy of conventional wisdom—were there beside me. Through the comfort of knowing that you had watched over me as I slept I would hear your voice whisper into my undefended dusk one single word: Home.

On the walk to school those mornings we would write songs and stories and I belonged.

Not at the school I attended.

Not at our church.

Not with the children I played with.

But with you.

Because of you home has been with me for every mile of my life's journey.

Thank you for the survival skills.

For the unique way of seeing the world.

For the ability to describe my world in a way that can resonate.

And for a home that knows no walls and from which I hopefully will not be evicted.

Show Me a Face

During her preschool years I would play a game with my daughter. I would say show me a happy face or a sad face and she would do her best to manufacture a countenance that under normal circumstances would appear naturally without forethought.

Later my requests required slightly deeper observational skills—show me an angry, frightened, or confused face.

By age eight our little game had advanced to the point where I would mark interactions that I observed at work and would reenact them for her after dinner.

"Me, you and our boss Bob are standing in a circle. Bob is lying to me. You know it. What does your face look like? No, that's much too dramatic. If your face looked like that we would know something was wrong. There may be times when you want the boss to know that you can see he's lying but today let's assume you don't. Try it again. Nope. Still too big. Here, look at my face. Watch. My face stays the same except I tighten my lips a little. I narrow my eyes just a tinge and the look in my eyes is not one that says there is a big problem. But if you look closely there is something in there that is slightly different than before I heard the lie."

When she was in middle school, my daughter would employ sophisticated, intricate, and often ingenious methods to avoid spending time with me. But periodically, despite her best efforts, we would find ourselves out in the world together. There, hidden, and thereby safe from the judgment of her friends she would let her guard down and we could have fun.

Parked in bustling Harvard Square with the windows rolled up we would create running commentary on all who walked by. Almost unrecognizable to the preschool version of our game, this was the advanced class. In this incarnation the rules are simple; say the first thing you think of about the people you see knowing that you will often be wrong. It's not about being right. It's about paying attention, being observant and getting your mind into the habit of thinking about what you are seeing and what it might mean. It's also a chance to indulge the irreverent brat in me (us).

"He likes her but she can't wait to get rid of him."

"Right. He's got his arm around her but her arm, hanging there by her side, is making a loud statement."

"This guy's from Everett. He came here to buy drugs."

"She's from a wealthy town. Great posture. She grew up in a house that didn't have any chairs that you could comfortably slouch in."

"Unslouchable chairs are the worst."

"I'd call it child abuse."

Observe. Think about what you observe. Make an educated guess at what your observation means. Store the information where you can call it up quickly if you need it. Be funny. Don't be afraid to be irreverent funny.

A Life Lesson from My Father

"Dad, I gotta ask you something. Why do you hang around with that guy? He's a drunk and a blowhard. He has no social skills. I've never left a conversation with him without thinking, 'I hope I never have to speak to that guy again.'"

"Ah, my son, my son. I'm going to give you a little life lesson. Just for the record, what I'm about to teach you, you should have learned on your own twenty years ago, but hey, better late than not at all.

"You are right about him, everything you said is true. I've been with him when other friends of mine would get up and leave the table because they couldn't stand to listen to another word he said. Not only does he think he knows everything but once he gets a few drinks in him he'll let you know how stupid he thinks you are in a way that makes you want to break a bottle over his head. But here is the thing young Don. I don't care about that. I've got a hundred friends that are charming and funny and everybody loves them. That's nice. I'm glad to have 'em. But if you came to me today and said you needed ten grand because one of your kids was sick or you were going to lose your house I'd call my obnoxious friend and that money would be in my hand in an hour.

"There is only one question: Can I count on you when it matters? If the answer is yes I don't give a rat's ass how you act or whether the rest of my friends go into a seizure at the sound of your name. Don't be a chump son. Charming friends that everyone likes are good to have. But when things get tough they are nowhere to be found. Pay attention. People will tell you everything you need to know about whether you can count on them or not by the way they act when they don't think you're watching."

When Joseph Larry (La-La) White was born in 1927 the future

was conspiring on multiple fronts to create a difficult childhood for him. The stock market crash that started the Great Depression happened two months and four days after his second birthday. Later, at age thirty, his father decided to have his first drink and almost instantly became the kind of drunk that would drink and gamble away his paycheck.

My dad was a first-born child of an alcoholic father who was raised by a single mom during the great depression.

Ponder that for a minute.

He was the one who should have written a book. But he didn't because spending time on an enterprise that couldn't produce immediate cash is a luxury that was not afforded to sons of Depression-era alcoholics. They went to work. When there was no work they stole stuff. When there was work they *still* stole stuff.

I don't want to get too deep into the survival skills employed by my dad in his youth. That is his story to tell and he is not here to tell it. When I walk through a graveyard I always think of the thousands of fascinating stories that are buried there. What it was really like for Dad to grow up in Lynn, Massachusetts without a father in the thirties and forties is a story that will live forever untold beneath the dirt in Pine Grove Cemetery. How it shaped him—how he went about navigating the world—is something we can talk about.

Let's start by taking a look at the word "winning." What does it mean to win? A child's understanding of winning is that you knock the opponent out and pound your chest so everyone can see how tough you are. What did you win? You won an enemy for life. Your supposed victory won you a person that will spend the rest of his days slandering you to everyone he knows resulting in hundreds of people that you *don't know* believing that you're a jerk. In return for a moment of chest-thumping glory you've created an invisible army that will never consider helping you and may actually work quietly against you. Winning to LaLa meant getting what you want without losing potential support from people you might need someday. The long game—my bloodline is wired to play it at a very high level.

Me and LaLa are first-born sons. I get him. I think like him. If I had known when I was an angry teenager that so many of my thoughts and survival skills were just updated versions of his I would have jumped off a bridge. But in my adult years this knowledge brings me great comfort. Not just because he's dead and I miss him. But because I can see now that the Larry White Long Game Method is a complex, sophisticated and powerful tool for navigating the world.

It starts with a strong inner voice. If you have one whose judgment you trust and you learn how to keep the noise of the world from separating you from hearing it, you have what my dad the Card Shark would call an ace in the hole—a reliable secret weapon.

Ponder this hypothetical but common scenario:

Both parents are alcoholics or drug-addicted. Their five children are feral. No one is raising them. No one is interested or capable of teaching them right from wrong. In fact, in addition to abdicating parental responsibilities, Mom and Dad frequently demean and humiliate their kids. Four of the children turn out the way one would expect with lots of problems and varying degrees of inability to function in the world. No surprise here. But one of the children not only turns out well, but also builds a life that embodies all the nurturing that he or she was denied as a child.

Why?

I have no idea.

But having no idea won't stop me from speculating in a way that sounds like I know what I'm talking about. I believe that these one-in-fivers, these against-all-odds-ers, these noteworthy statistical outliers all have a strong inner voice that they trust and defend. I also believe that these folks learn to question what they see around them and trust what they hear inside them.

These days when I meet someone that I can't figure out—someone that I'm not quite comfortable around or I'm not sure I can trust—I can hear my dad whispering to me. "Let this donkey (he loved calling people donkeys) keep talking. Be quiet. Pay attention. What he says and does when he doesn't think anyone is watching will tell you everything you need to know about him. Then put that information in your ass pocket. (Ass pocket is a 1940s term for database.) And just hold on to it. You may never need it. But if you do it'll be there and you can use it to stay ahead of the game if that's what the situation requires. Always have an ace in the hole son."

1989: Legion Hall

My dad was kind, smart, empathetic, funny, and generous of spirit. Sometimes on Christmas morning we would wake up to find a stranger sleeping on our couch. Dad always tended bar on Christmas Eve because the tips were good. His customers would all be men who lived in rooming houses who just wanted to avoid for as long as possible being alone on Christmas. Due to the preponderance of empty pockets in his youth LaLa's primary driving force in his adult life was to make and hang on to money. But just beneath that was a deep sense of empathy. The challenges of his youth only strengthened his ability to put himself in other people's shoes. My siblings and I grew up with it being perfectly normal to have Christmas dinner with an unshaven stranger because "no one should be alone on Christmas."

Larry White was a fantastic bartender. He was a true showman. Watching him tend bar was spellbinding. He understood that he was on a stage, that it was a show and that the audience was made up of working-class veterans who loved sardonic repartee. (They wouldn't call it that even if they could because in the local dialect the term "talking shit" would be correct. Anything else would be deemed pompous.)

Before I left Lynn I thought everyone had as deep and reverent an appreciation for flippancy as the White family. Imagine my surprise when the type of irreverent humor that would have my friends and family laughing so hard they were squirting out a little pee (an accomplishment that has become a lot easier as friends and family have aged) would be viewed as insensitive.

"Insensitive? Are you kidding me? What a buncha babies." That is what always goes through my mind when I deliver a Larry White type joke to a room full of Unitarians and instead of laughing they convene an emergency meeting. "Is it okay to laugh at this? Is he making fun of an oppressed segment of society? Was that a little sexist? Let's have a show of hands to see if we agree that it is okay to laugh at this."

Over time I have slowly come to realize that most Americans were not raised in a factory town near Boston by two wisecracking punks. Now I get it. I feel bad for all the fun you're missing but I get it. You're nice.

Larry knew his audience. He had stock comebacks that he would use like "Before I started working here I was six foot two and blonde." He would listen to someone engaged in barstool pontifications and then, if there were women present, he would call the pontificator "soft as a grape." If his clientele were only men he would pull out the Boston-est of all his favorite insults and call him "soft as a sneaker full of shit."

Larry died before political correctness could take anything from him. I know now that it is inconsiderate to call someone crazy and I try not to do it because my heart is big and I don't want to hurt anyone. But I cannot describe to you how deeply I mourn the loss of this term. Barely a day goes by when I don't ache to proclaim that a friend, family member or politician is soft as a sneaker full of shit.

Our family's hearts are generous and our empathy is immense. It will be there when you need it but you won't see it till then. We don't wear it on our sleeves. If you're from a place where people are open and sweet and you're trying to figure us out, here is a good rule of thumb: If we're making fun of you— that means we like you. If we're quiet ... you really should leave.

*****

I make a living because I write songs and stories and perform them for audiences. The route to making money in this manner has taken me the wrong way down one-way streets and to more than a few cul-de-sacs where my career would spin in a small circle—sometimes for years.

Looking back I can see that at every point of stagnation I would default to what I learned growing up the son of a hard drinker in a working class factory town:

1) Be stubborn and unreasonable.
2) Ignore good advice from well-intentioned and knowledgeable friends.
3) Make every effort to do the things that people smarter than you say never to do.
4) And try to be as much of an asshole as possible to everyone that only wants the best for you.

I could argue that my bratty unreasonableness has contributed more to my ability to make a living as a performer than my songwriting or comedy skills. Someone smarter might argue that these impulsive behaviors are why it took so long to get here. I would, of course, apply rule number four to that argument and walk away leaving a trail of palpable disdain in my wake.

The music business eats its young. The road to making your first dollar as a performer is more like a gauntlet where you either surrender your dreams or learn how to persevere while being ignored, disrespected, and occasionally booed. We children of alcoholics, having early on built impenetrable walls around our hearts to defend our vulnerability, are uniquely qualified to survive the comparatively unimpressive disrespect of said gauntlet.

In the 1980s being my booking agent was an exercise in rejection. I burned through three or four of them that decade. If you ever find yourself in a place where all your labor produces satisfying results and you need a little balance in your life you should try cold-calling overworked, underpaid venue owners on behalf of an artist they never heard of who couldn't draw five people to their club. That'll cure ya.

Since no one would hire me, I hired myself. Twice a year I rented the function hall at the American Legion where my Dad was a member. I assembled a band of local musicians. I hung up posters, sent out mailings, rented lights and sound and locked the door behind me when I left.

After a particularly wild and successful show I was standing in the back of the hall with a group of friends and family. "What a great show Don. When is the next one? I have a friend at work who would love this." Just then a friend walked up and said, "Don, your dad is shitfaced. He's in the men's room talking to himself." My brother and a family friend soon emerged on either side of LaLa holding him upright as best they could drunk-walking him toward the door while he waved one arm in the air performing his "fuck you" show. "Fuck you ... mumble, mumble, Fuucck You."

Then he fell and knocked over a rectangular banquet table with twenty empty beer bottles on it. The sound was spectacular. It reverberated all the way back to my childhood.

The Oblivious Expert

The look on my mother's face as my brother and my friend picked Larry up and walked him out of the hall is as clear in my mind now as it was all those years ago. She was traumatized. She knew that I had worked for months to put the show together and that there was no real money to be made—that my only compensation were the compliments I was accruing before the Larry scene.

She saw that the moment changed the conversation from "That was a great show" to "Sorry about your Dad." She saw, as is so common for children of alcoholics, that I had been ripped off—that my summer labors would not bring in the harvest.

I felt nothing.

I would have sworn on the lives of my children that there was no problem. "He's a drunk. This is what that looks like. Why are you all being such babies about this?"

She said to me, "you need to talk to him about his drinking. He won't listen to me. He'll listen to you."

And then, in a moment that epitomizes the obliviousness within which my life at the time resided, I said, "Sure. I'll talk to him. No big deal."

I told my mother that I would take a week and do a little research and think about it before I talked to Dad. My sister and I agreed to attend a couple of al-anon meetings. I would talk to some friends with experience in these matters and I would speak with him the following Sunday.

Alcohol is an equal opportunity employ/destroy-er. It does not discriminate. It destroys an equal percentage of lives across the board. There are just as many alcoholic plumbers as professors, tough guys as not tough guys, men, women, Catholics, Jews, and atheists. To me it's like a parasitic virus looking for a host. It is wholly unconcerned about the unique contributions the potential host is participating *in* and contributing *into* the lives of other non-parasites. Warm blood is the only essential prerequisite. A family history or a predisposition to alcoholism is helpful but the absence of either is not a deal breaker.

My grandfather lost his job and his family through alcohol. Larry, on the other hand, retired with over forty years' service at the General Electric plant and with his family intact. He had a pension, excellent medical coverage, and a six-room house with a white picket fence with no mortgage. Frequent consumption of whiskey was something he and my grandfather had in common. The tangible results and effect on their respective families were very different.

I grew up knowing I was loved. No one ever abandoned, demeaned, or beat me. I do not have the kind of stories to tell that would have caused anyone to be concerned for my well-being physically or otherwise.

The fact that my upbringing is void of the predictability one would find in virtually any and all television movies on the subject of growing up the son of a hard drinker is what makes it interesting to me. The story is not in the police record because there isn't one. The story is under the surface. It is complex, nuanced, and rarely rises to a crescendo. Instead it is buried deep inside the way that the steady slow burn of the situation shaped my survival skills.

At the time of the Legion Hall incident I was decades into a master class in conflict aversion via accelerated observational skills. At the time I would have given credit to having grown up in a working-class neighborhood and the fact that my wife and I hitchhiked around North America for the better part of three years in the seventies for these advanced skills. But today as I tell this story I think that being the first-born son of a man with a drinking problem probably started the process long before I went to school and was exposed to bullies.

Today I'm thinking that my brain, even its early formative years, was engaged in very sophisticated maneuverings and manipulations to protect my little boy heart.

Pinch Hit Grand Slam

During the week that followed my mother's injunction I did some reading on what smart people had to say about adult children of alcoholics and what methods they in their smartness would use to confront the boozer in the family.

A quiet part of me knew that this due diligence was required but the louder part of me thought, "I'll go over there right now and tell him that he shouldn't drink so much and that will be it." However, as the week went on and the date of the confrontation got closer the quiet voice got steadily … measurably louder.

It kept arguing that I shouldn't be so attached to the Sunday deadline, which it called arbitrary. It kept saying, "Blow this thing off till next week. What's your hurry? He's been a drunk since forever what's another week going to change?"

I responded by demanding to know why Sunday wasn't good enough. The fact that Mr. Increasingly Loud Bossy Voice pretended not to hear my question and kept offering suggestions on how to delay the confrontation activated the stubborn brat in me.

For reasons much too complex for a product of the Lynn Public School system to decipher, the core of me is viscerally resistant to being told what to do. When the command doesn't feel the need to justify itself with even a fabricated reason the cold steel plate between what I am being ordered to do and my agreeing to do it is one hundred percent impenetrable.

I cannot recall one example where I have acquiesced under these circumstances.

Tell me why or shut up.

*****

On Saturday night I walked past my daughter's bedroom. She was sitting on the floor playing a video game (Nintendo).

I stood in the hallway thinking "I have talked to my son and my wife about my situation with my dad but I always think of my daughter as too young to include in complicated matters. Maybe, just out of courtesy, I should brief her."

I turned around, walked back to her room and asked her to pause the game and sit on the bed with me.

"I want to include you in something that has been going on with me this past week. Sometimes I still think of you as the baby here but you're almost eight now and that's old enough to be kept in the loop like everyone else.

"My dad drinks too much and your grandmother asked me to talk to him about it. When she first asked me I didn't think it would be very hard. But now that I have to do it tomorrow morning I'm kinda scared. I don't know if I will say it the right way or if it will hurt his feelings or if it will change my relationship with him. I love him a lot and I only want what's best for him and for my mom. So I just wanted to tell you that if you've noticed that I've been a little distracted this week, that is the reason."

I was thinking to myself that I had just done a pretty cool dad thing. I was patting myself on the back and in my mind I was starting work on the first draft of my Father of the Year acceptance speech.

The truth, as it is so often, was opposite my perception. I wasn't including my daughter because I respected her opinion. As the observant reader will note, I spoke my piece and was preparing to leave. It never crossed my mind to think that she might have something useful or interesting to say. The entire scene was obligatory. It was like she was the last kid picked for the baseball team. I was doing the nice thing by making her feel included but I was still putting her in right field where no balls were likely to be hit.

Before I could rise from the bed in my self-congratulatory delusion she said, "I know exactly how you feel." It startled me. It was the last thing a coach expected to hear from a little league right fielder that he was sure would spend the game chasing butterflies with her glove on the wrong hand.

I sat back on the bed and said, "You do?" "Yes. Remember back when Mom used to smoke cigarettes? Well, she used to hide it from us. So, one morning I got up early and I caught her smoking in the kitchen. She tried to hide it under the table but I saw it and I smelled the smoke. I ran upstairs to my room. I was so upset." She waved her arm with a pointed index finger from the floor by the door to the window at the far end of the room and said, "I walked back and forth in here for a long time. I wanted to tell her that smoking was bad for her lungs and that it could kill her. But I was afraid to do it. But after a while I forced myself to go back downstairs. I told her how bad it was and how much I hated that she smoked. And she quit smoking that day."

She picked up the remote control and sat on the floor. Her back was to me and her legs were crossed beneath her boney butt.

Before she unpaused the video game she turned her head around and said, "I know exactly how you feel. It will be really hard. You'll probably cry. But when it's over you'll be glad you didn't chicken out."

My seven-year-old guru daughter had distilled down to two paragraphs what smarty pants counselors take hundreds of pages to say. I sat there stunned while the Nintendo Mario Brothers music played the scene to a close.

Let's Get This Over With

On Sunday morning thirty-four-year-old Don White woke up eleven-year-old Donnie White with a gentle touch to the shoulder. He whispered, "It's time to get this over with little man."

In the time it took for young Donnie to transition from dream to day his eyes betrayed the vulnerability and primal fear visible only in the fleeting seconds before his conscious mind would find its footing and put on its emotional suit of armor. I acknowledged the story that those transitional eyes told and watched as it once again hid behind the no fear, no empathy, nothing-can-hurt-me eyes of a runaway sixth grader.

Each night when I slip into dreamland a cleaning crew goes to work in my mind and starts sweeping and mopping up all the useless crap that I accrued during the day. My brain is like a giant storage locker—where I pay to store unnecessary and often detrimental stuff that my conscious mind is afraid to part with.

Picture these guys coming to work every night, standing just inside the entry door, looking around and saying, "What a mess. We're gonna be here all damn night. He must have overdosed on coffee today. Charlie, see that gigantic pile of over-caffeinated, unnecessary worry in the corner? Throw it in the dumpster. Jimmy, you start sweeping up all that career stress. The rest of you take a mop and bucket to all the other crap this poor fool spent his day stuffing into this locker as if some day it might be worth something."

When morning is pulling into the parking lot he sees the crew leaning on their respective brooms and mops. They are admiring their work and acknowledging that if conscious me ever evolved to the point where he was filling his storage unit with nice shiny positive thoughts these guys would all become unemployed.

*****

During the five-minute drive to Abbott Street for the Don/Dad confrontation Mister Increasing Louder Bossy Voice was losing it. All week long, even though he had gradually amped up his volume, he had been able to maintain a firm but constrained tone. But now he spoke with fevered desperation. The fact that we were minutes away from the situation he had worked so hard to prevent blew apart his veneer of calm. He was yelling. "Go get a cup of coffee! Go sit somewhere and read the paper! Collect your damn thoughts! This does not have to happen today!"

I responded with steel-eyed venom and equal volume. "Tell me why or shut up!" I was not going to be talked out of this without a valid reason. Not because I thought confronting my dad about his drinking was a great idea. But because before the cement of my personality's foundation had hardened, circum-stances introduced into its soft mortar the survival skill of stub-born resistance to unreasonableness.

Responding to the type of authority that is disinclined to reasonably defend its commands with a more tenacious degree of unreasonableness is an irony that is not lost on me.

I am not defending who I was and how I behaved. From the lofty perch of age sixty-four my actions back then look exactly like what you would expect from a man in his thirties who hadn't acquired (but would momentarily) the following important knowledge: The armor you build to protect your heart from feeling the trauma that you experience separates your head from your heart so effectively that it actually saves your life. If decades go by and you don't get behind there and feel all that crap when it is safe to do so, it screws up your life without you knowing how or why.

The thing that saves your life during a traumatic experience slowly destroys your life if left in place too long.

More on this later.

Halfway to the house I was raised in—where all my ghosts lived—I was fully engaged in a screaming match with that infuriating renegade hunk of my mind. I could feel the power aligned against the fulfillment of this job. I knew if I let my guard down for one minute it would wear down my formidable counterattack. So I drove as fast as I could. I came to a screeching halt in front of the house. I ran at full speed down the driveway with the inside of my head screaming at me at full volume, "STOP! YOU HAVE NO IDEA WHAT YOU ARE ABOUT TO UNLEASH!" And me screaming back, "SHUT UP, SHUT UP SHUT UP. I DON'T CARE WHAT YOU SAY OR HOW LOUD YOU SAY IT. I AM DOING THIS NOW!"

When I put my hand on the knob of the door that would open up to the kitchen of my youth, my mind became abruptly silent. My stubborn rage instantly changed to fear—a fear so primal that it buckled my knees. The part of me that had access to the emotional magnitude of what was about to transpire said "good luck friend" and walked down the driveway toward the street. Later when I thought back on this moment I pictured my noble cleaning crew talking in the locker room like the baseball team who had a great season but just lost the World Series. "There's no reason to feel bad about this. We did everything humanly possible. It was a herculean effort. His stubbornness just proved to be a little too strong for us. There's nothing to be ashamed of here boys. Get some rest. That storage unit is going to be a catastrophe tonight."

I pushed the door open and found myself in the same kitchen and in the exact spot where I had stood with a priest beside me in 1968. The dam was breached. The water was coming.

I never felt more alone.

Ambush

My Dad was a short and wide barrel-chested man. He was eating breakfast at the far end of the kitchen table wearing the type of shoulder-strapped t-shirt that in his day no one ever thought twice about calling a wife beater.

For the next full minute he sat frozen in time holding a fork with a portion of scrambled eggs locked at shoulder height en route to his mouth. Later he told me that by the look on my face that day he thought that one of my kids had died.

When I opened my mouth the lava that had been hidden beneath the unknowing calm of Mount Don for decades erupted thousands of feet into the atmosphere and melted everything.

I was screaming and crying. "You need to know how your drinking has affected everyone in this family! I never felt safe. I had to grow up too fast. You loved us second. Drinking was your number one love. Why should I have all these memories of waking up to a drunken horror show?"

At one point I stood there pointing at an imaginary hole in the ground screaming, "I'm not going to wait till you're dead to say this stuff to a casket. I'm saying it now. Your drinking has messed up everyone in this house. You need to know it and you need to do something about it now!"

A little piece of scrambled egg fell in slow motion from the fork that was still suspended in mid-air. There was a four-second silence during which I could see him making sense out of what had just happened. He needed that time. This was an ambush. Not only did he not see it coming but he didn't even know there was a problem—at least not one with the volcanic urgency that had just lava'd his breakfast.

Finally he said, "Okay, I'll try to stop drinking." I said "Okay" and walked out the door.

Snapshots

All the ways I had navigated my world from childhood were standing on the sidewalk in front of the house as I climbed into the van and pulled away. They looked like buggy whip makers staring in through the window at the first Model T assembly line. They got smaller and smaller in my rearview mirror until they disappeared and were consigned to history.

At home I brewed a cup of tea and sat on my back porch. My wife sat beside me as I stared through the steam. "How'd it go?" I was unable to answer ... well, unwilling to answer. It wasn't the right question. The right question was being asked over and over on a loop in my mind. "What happens now?" As I write this on a plane ride to Detroit twenty-seven years later I have a complete and complex answer but at that moment I only knew that I had just knocked down a fortified wall that had protected me since childhood. My heart was racing. It was the same feeling I had when I was sent to the principal's office in the fifth grade and had to wait on a bench in the hallway until he called me into his office to pass judgment on my crimes and then dispense justice. I knew it was going to be bad but I didn't know if it would be call-my-mother-to-come-get-me bad or a level I could navigate like a note describing my felonies that I could forge her signature on. Even though I couldn't gauge the power and fury of what was coming I couldn't shake the unsettling feeling that my ability to navigate it would prove inadequate.

Before the airing of my grievances with my dad I had a lot of memories that were like snapshots. Whenever they surfaced I would hold them in my hand like old polaroid photos. There were no feelings attached to them. I would look at each one, feel nothing, and put it away.

The next morning, thirty minutes into a two-hour ride to a job in Springfield, my mind began attempting to grasp the magnitude of what had transpired the day before. Just beyond Route 495, where the traffic had thinned out, a familiar snapshot came to mind. It was 1967. I was ten years old and obsessed with baseball to a degree that today would be diagnosed as compulsive and treated with medication. My little league team was in the final rounds of the playoffs. There was one game left. The winning team would be league champions. I had been an infielder all season but because we had played three games the previous week the rules wouldn't allow any of our pitchers to take the mound in this final championship game. So I was recruited to pitch. I was nervous all the way to the center of my preadolescent solar plexus. The biggest game of the year with the whole season on the line and I have to pitch? I'm a shortstop dammit! This is crazy.

The day before the game I wanted my dad to play catch with me. He wouldn't. My mother, who was forever trying to do the right thing, had grabbed a catcher's mitt and we threw the ball in the front yard. I hated it. It just felt so wrong. I didn't want to hurt her feelings but man what a mess. She'd never played base-ball in her life. She was left-handed and the righty glove looked stupid on her.

While my mom and I were playing the world's most dys-functional game of catch my dad came out of the house, walked past us, got into his gigantic white Plymouth Fury and drove off. He was going to the bar at the Legion Hall to be with, as far as my young and unworldly mind could determine, the thing he really loved, which was *not me*. I felt like every window in every house on Abbott Street had a neighbor looking out of it watch-ing a real-time portrayal of how screwed up my family was.

This memory had been popping up in my head for over twenty years. I never had a single feeling about it. Nothing. It was like a photograph of something that happened to someone I didn't care about.

Well boys and girls, this time the cold blue steel wall that I had built in my youth to separate my heart from my childhood traumas had been blown to pieces by my irrational decision to confront my father about his drinking less than twenty-four hours before. And for the first time in my life I felt *everything*. Not just everything that I could have/should have felt at the moment it happened but all of that multiplied by the twenty-plus years it had been down there brewing in a secret cauldron behind my impenetrable defense system.

I don't think it's an exaggeration to say it nearly killed me. It certainly felt like there was a chance I wouldn't survive the gigantic wave of emotion that washed over me as I was driving sixty-five miles per hour somewhere near Worcester.

I started crying the kind of cry that babies sometimes do when they are half-convulsing and gasping for air. I pulled the car over beside a guardrail on a curve. Truck drivers were blowing their horns and giving me the finger. I was out of my mind. I kept saying, out loud through convulsions and gasps, "No wonder people don't confront this stuff! This sucks! I'm such a stubborn idiot! I could easily have gone all the way to Pine Grove Cemetery without feeling any of this!"

Then a truly terrifying realization came to me: "I've got dozens of these memories!!! I'm going to have to *feel* all of them!"

The Power of Funny

On Christmas Day 2019 the whole family was gathered at our house for the last time. My wife and I were getting too old to continue hosting. Our house was too small to accommodate the growing family and we were too old.

Did I already say that we were too old?

Yes?

There's your proof.

I was sitting in the living room drinking in the sounds—marking the moment. Everyone was laughing. This is a funny family. We take our humor seriously. We try to be kind to other people who think they're funny. But there is always a touch of condescension in the modest chuckles we give to those we perceive as apprentices. If you listen closely you can hear "nice try, keep working on it" underneath our polite laughter. We're comedy snobs. We can't help it.

Many people have asked me if anyone can learn to get a laugh. My answer is yes. I have taught some very dour humans to tell a joke well. It's a good side business for me. And it's totally teachable no matter what anyone who espouses the you're-either-funny-or-you're-not view of comedy says. There's no magic to it. Once she has some basic knowledge about misdirection and a half dozen other easily understandable comedy basics even your morose aunt will be able to effectively tell a joke.

But … getting a modest laugh via a comedy formula and making a room of people erupt into laughter with something spontaneous are two entirely different species of animal.

My family breeds in-the-moment funny.

I have twin grandsons who are eleven years old. Studying the evolution of their ability to comprehend and deliver humor has given me a new appreciation for the complexities and multi-generational breeding that goes into the creation of a quick-witted comedy mind.

When you grow up with what the outside world would call naturally funny people you are drawn at a very young age to the power of laughter. Children always know where the center of attention is and are pulled toward it. Bring a four-year-old to a folk concert and see how long it takes for that child to be standing on or directly in front of the stage. So, anyone who grows up around laughter will see how it gets the attention of everyone in the room. It's only natural to become driven to figure out how to make your family laugh and get some of that attention—even before you are able to speak in complete sentences.

How does that saying go? You never want to see how sausage or laws are made? I would add comedian to that list. It takes a whole lot of awkward moments to get from not funny to off-the-cuff funny.

The first things the twins laughed at were funny sounds—fart noises especially. (Wait till they figure out that you can ask Alexa to make one.) A few years later they started to understand how words can have two meanings. Did you ever see a fishbowl—fish bowl? They would laugh themselves silly with knock knock jokes and other humor that didn't require any worldliness to understand. The first time I began to think that they were entering the next phase was when they laughed at this joke: Why do whales love to swim in salt water? Because pepper water makes them sneeze. A kindergartener will probably not laugh at this joke because they'll miss the connection between salt and pepper. But a second grader gets it.

From the age of seven to eleven there were a whole lot of failed attempts by my grandchildren to make me laugh. But they were tenacious. They never quit. They never thought about quitting. These descendants of Don and Larry White were going to learn how to be the person getting the family to laugh if it took twenty years.

*****

I suddenly feel the need to explain to you what's going on here. So, a few pages back we had just completed a couple of pretty dramatic chapters in the story about my relationship with my dad. And now I can feel you wondering what on Earth this essay on comedy has to do with any of that? The answer is nothing— well, almost nothing.

Think of it as a bit of a breather. Writing about all this family stuff is exhausting. It makes me all weepy and blank-stare-out-the-window-y. That's why it's taking so long to finish this thing. Today is Jan 11th 2020. I finished Chapter 9 in June 2019. How long will it take to finish a story of say, seventeen chapters if the author takes seven months off between each one?

Anyway, I *am* going to finish this thing and I *am* going to tie this comedy digression back into the overall arc of the story in a way that will be almost justifiable. The point is that I need a breather and I like talking about comedy. And since it is likely that I shan't be putting pen to parchment for another book I'm wedging this thing in here.

I was sitting on the couch with one of the twins and I decided that we should rewrite the lyrics to Doe a Deer. I said, "Dough—some bread that's not cooked yet. Ray"—he said, "the gun I use in space."

It didn't make me laugh but it wasn't bad.

Eventually we got to La.

Let's take a minute and talk about the La line in the original song. To me that line is the biggest abdication of lyric writing responsibility in the entire history of songwriting.

La—a note to follow sol.

Really?

It's like they already got paid for the job and just quit.

In 1972 Alice Cooper wrote this lyric: "We got no class and we got no principles and we got no innocence. We can't even think of a word that rhymes."

I like that. It's malicious. It fits the attitude of the School's Out For Summer motif.

A note to follow sol? Give me a break. They just threw in the towel, took the money and went out drinking.

I said "La" and my grandson said, "It comes before de da!"

I laughed out loud. I looked at him in amazement. I remembered the first time I made my dad laugh and how life-changing it was for me. We stood there and marked the moment. I took the crown off my head and placed it gently upon his noble dome. In our family this was the equivalent of his bar mitzvah.

Later, I was at the table with the other twin. He was telling me a story. When he finished I said, "I think you're fibbing. I'm going to take my de-*fib*ulator and type in what you said and if it's a fib a bell will ring and it will print out a paper document that proves you were fibbing." So I started typing on my imaginary device. I said, "ding ding ding." I tore off an invisible piece of paper, handed it to him and said, "yup, that was a fib."

My grandson grabbed the make-believe device, pulled it over in front of him and started typing. I said, "What are you doing?" To which he replied, "I'm typing the word defibulator into this thing." Then he said "ding ding ding," ripped of an invisible document, handed it to me and said, "Your defibulator says there's no such thing as a defibulator."

Wow.

Then came the moment when I knew that we as a family were about to unleash a highly evolved mutant strain of funny into an unsuspecting world. My son was trying unsuccessfully to herd his three proverbial cats (i.e., kids). He said (playfully), "If you don't put your shoes on I'm going to scream." I asked, "Will it be a Christmas scream?" And then an eleven-year-old newly anointed comedian looked up from a game he was playing on the living room floor and sang "Oh Christmas scream, oh Christmas scream how lovely are thy branches." The whole family—cousins, uncles, aunts, and grandparents—laughed and then stood in silence. It wasn't gut-busting funny but, we all knew that it was quick-witted and spontaneous. It was a new development. A threshold had just been crossed. We had just collectively learned that the journey from birth to wiseass in our bloodline now takes less than twelve years.

In the reverent quiet that followed we gave silent thanks to all the witty jokesters of the family that had gone before us upon whose irreverent shoulders we were standing.

I could write a book on humor and laughter. I'm not going to. I'm already sick of writing this book. People my age who love to write books are mystifying to me. Yes, it can be intoxicating to be wrapped up in your own mind for hour upon hour every day. But how do you justify spending months of your life documenting your old memories while the sun rises and sets on your diminishing opportunities to create new ones? The adventures I didn't have today because I spent six hours telling you about my past adventures are like babies that will never be born. Writing a book is new memory contraception.

That last line made me go take a walk in Lynn Woods.

Okay, where was I?

Humor and laughter.

Of all the fascinating things there are to learn about the healing power of laughter the one I find most compelling comes in the aftermath of irreverent or dark humor.

In my family the more pressure we're under the funnier we become. Put us in a situation where solemnity reigns and we will burst its bubble. Church is a good example. Or if you ever have the misfortune to be at a funeral with us, you will hate us. It's not intentional. We're not trying to be disrespectful. We just don't know any other way to break the tension.

At a funeral someone we love is laid out. People are crying. We want to cry but that is not going to happen. At the exact moment that any one of us feels tears welling up someone will break the tension with humor. We know it infuriates you but on behalf of my family going back a hundred years I just want to state clearly here that we don't care about you. We're just trying to take care of ourselves and this is the way we do it. I guess you could say that the White family puts the f u n back in funeral.

It is quite an evolutionary accomplishment to take this thing—humor—that only human beings are capable of, and use it strategically to open a valve and let the steam whistle out before the pipe breaks.

Digressing to the Point of No Return

Twenty years before he died my father got pneumonia. He wanted to treat it like a hangover.

I said, "Dad, Alka-Seltzer ain't gonna cure pneumonia. You have to go to the doctor."

"I hate the doctor. I'll be fine."

"Who's your primary care physician?"

"I don't know. I was stationed in Norfolk, Virginia when I was in the navy. Some guy in a white coat stuck a bunch of needles in my ass before they sent us overseas—was that him?"

"No dad, that was not your primary care physician."

He hadn't seen a doctor in twenty years. He hadn't cracked a sweat since World War Two. He hadn't eaten a vegetable since the fifties. He ate red bloody meat and boiled potatoes, smoked two packs of cigarettes every day, drank Seagram's Seven whiskey and constantly dared his lifestyle choices to kill him. When he was eighty years old he said to me in a voice permanently graveled by tobacco,

"Donnie, I found a new fried clam place."

"Dad, what did your doctor say about eating fried clams?"

"My doctor? You mean the one that told me to stop eating fried clams?"

"Yes."

"He died twenty years ago. If you want to live to be eighty you gotta ignore what your doctor says and do what you want. C'mon let's go get some clams."

The pneumonia'd version of Larry White was not going to be easily persuaded to go to the emergency room. He had given the middle finger to every single thing that ever had the audacity to threaten his life and invariably he continued living while the thing that tried to kill him died. Why would pneumonia be different?

But it was different. His skin was ashen. He was dying and needed to be made aware of the fact that he had finally encountered a worthy opponent.

My brother and I stood on either side of his bed and calmly explained the seriousness of his situation. "We're all worried about you. This is not like other stuff. Your breathing is weak. Your skin is turning gray. You keep falling asleep mid-sentence. You've got a family here that loves you. We all love you Dad. You have to go to the emergency room."

Larry White from Wyman Street looked up from his bed with eyes moist with love and appreciation. He said, "That was beautiful. I always hoped that my children would grow up to be good caring people. I can see now how much you care and that you only want what's best for me. You will never know how much that means to me.

"Now fuck off."

The ease with which those last three words rolled off his tongue was more than impressive. It was effortless and a thing of beauty. Although we didn't laugh out loud we knew it was funny and he was still the king. Even when he was mostly dead.

After another hour of watching our well-reasoned and heartfelt pleas swatted away with a doctorate level of sarcasm followed by a smirk of glee we knew that we were hopelessly outmatched and outgunned. We would have to call in our secret weapon.

Twenty minutes later our sister Diane arrived. If you want to know how she deals with the small challenges in her life you'd have to ask her kids or her husband. I don't live with her so I don't know. But when it counts—when someone in the bloodline is in trouble—she's a force of nature.

"What's going on?"

"We think he's got pneumonia. His lungs are all gurgl-y. Ma

says he's been nodding off mid-sentence for a few days and he won't go to the emergency room."

"Okay. I got this. Warm up the car."

If Larry were Samson, Superman, or Achilles our baby sister would be hair scissors, kryptonite, or a knife wound to the tendon.

Larry's bedroom was at the top of the stairs. Diane's powers over him were so absolute that she didn't even need to go into his room. She stood three steps from the top and barked at him. "In my whole life I've never asked you for anything. I'm asking you now to get out of that bed and go to the emergency room." There was no argument. He got up, got dressed and came downstairs. My dad may well have been the toughest, most stubborn, person I ever knew but in the hands of his only daughter he was downright pliable.

On the drive to the hospital he was smoking a cigarette. In between inhalations he would cough and complain. "I don't need a doctor, cough, hack, cough. I'll be all right in a couple of days." He went on that way for about five minutes until my sister burned two holes in his forehead with a glare that unveiled her unmitigated authority.

I'm writing this while under lockdown during the coronavirus outbreak of 2020. When my parents were alive there was actually a hospital and an emergency room in our town. Today, when we need it the most, there is not. The reason I am living in a hospital-less city of ninety thousand people during a global pandemic is that the healthcare of my community was sold to corporate interests by corrupt politicians.

Where was I?

Oh yeah, Larry's trip to the emergency room.

The ER waiting room was busy when we arrived. We expected to wait a long time. When the glass doors opened the head nurse—a no-nonsense, seen-everything, forty-something authoritarian—spotted us. She pointed an extended index finger at Larry and said, "You, the old bastard with the cigarette, come here."

She took him into a room and put a device on his finger that measures the oxygen in your blood. She took it off, looked at it, shook it a bit, flicked it a couple of times with her middle finger and then said, "Mr. White, according to this, you're dead. But since you don't have the good sense to fall down we have a nice bed for you up in intensive care."

Hours later everyone had left except my brother and me. He was on one side of the bed and I was on the other. Larry was unconscious. He had a tube stuffed down his throat that was forcing air into his lungs to get his oxygen levels up beyond the just-this-side-of-cadaver levels he had been walking around and smoking Marlboros with for a week. He was hooked up to all manner of tubes and wires connected to beeping boxes and bags of fluid. He was on morphine. Apparently there is some kind of hospital rule about the family not having any. My brother and I figured it was worth asking about but the answer was a firm indignant "no." Only Larry was getting any morphine this day.

As you can see I'm having a little fun at my dad's expense here. Again, just my way of breaking the tension. Don't get me wrong. I loved that guy. I can make a living as a performer on stage because I was able to monetize his wit and his mischief and the playful charm of his worldview. His view of the world was "be yourself, let them deal with it." Please don't mistake my use of humor in the telling of this part of the story as disrespect. I was heartbroken. They were telling us that he might not live through the night. We were thinking that we were saying goodbye to him.

I guess you could say that there was a lot of pressure on my brother and me. And as we have learned, the more pressure you put my family under, the funnier we become.

My brother Mike has the quickest comedy wit I have ever known. He will just quip something out from the side of his mouth at the dinner table and everyone will know that it was the funniest thing that anyone on earth could have said at that moment. I have been stealing his off-the-cuff material and polishing it up for use in my concerts for decades.

So there we were standing on opposite sides of the bed while the barrel chest of this man we love was rising and falling from forced air. It was one of the most serious moments two siblings could share.

My brother aimed his icy blues eyes at me and in a solemn tone with a voice just above a whisper he said, "Ma told him to stop smoking. He didn't listen." I replied with equal solemnity, "That's right, Michael. She did tell him to quit smoking and he just wouldn't listen." Then he said, "Ma told him to quit drinking. He didn't listen." "I know, she did tell him to quit drinking and he did not listen." Then my brother, with a tear in his eye said, "The one time she tells him to drop dead, he listens."

And we laughed. We laughed so hard it hurt. I felt my knees buckle. Water was pouring out of my eyes and I was gasping for air. I thought to myself, I might have to rip that tube out of my dad and use it myself. That increased my laughing fit. I felt all the pressure—all the my-heart-feels-like-it-is-going-to-burst pressure—fly out of my body. Irreverent, dark humor saved my life that day.

A nurse came to the door to see what all the hysteria was about. I remember her standing there with a bewildered look on her face thinking, "What is wrong with these people?" I couldn't tell her that she was witnessing the aftermath of what is probably the most highly evolved self-healing technique on earth.

Larry lived.

Fifteen years later we were at my mother's funeral.

*****

My mother Photini "Frannie" Sotiropolous White was born in the wrong time. She was destined to be a rebel. She would have gone to Woodstock. She would have hitchhiked around the country. She would have followed The Grateful Dead. Unfortunately, she graduated from high school in the mid-forties and there was nobody to be a rebel with. So she did the best she could as sort of a freelance lone wolf rebel.

The nineteen seventies would have been perfect for my mother's late teens or early twenties. Even though her children's behavior during those years caused her lots of worry I know she envied us. There was a look in her eye when she watched my generation flaunt their independence in the face of waning social mores within which you could see the omnipotent oppression of the free-spirited kids of the 1940s.

She didn't like anyone that was mean but if you were a good kid that liked to be in and around trouble she loved you. If you had run away from home or escaped from juvenile hall or were getting chased by the police she'd take you in. Our house was like the Underground Railroad for wayward children. You could hide there until Mom decided whether or not to call your parents. The price for sanctuary with us was that you had to tell my mother the detailed story of your adventures outside the law. During my teenage years Mom lived vicariously through my rotten friends. And being the good son that I am, I accrued a tremendous amount of rotten friends for my mother to hang around with.

She would listen intently and drink in every morsel of these stories as if they were feeding her the nutrients of rebellion that she was denied as a child of the thirties and forties.

At her funeral all the grown-up versions of my delinquent friends showed up. The room was like an advertisement for day passes and work release programs.

My mother was Greek but not especially religious. Her sisters demanded that we have the deacon from the Greek Orthodox church come and talk ... and talk ... and talk some more and keep on talking and not stop talking and talk some more and NOT STOP TALKING.

Our family was seated at the front of the room against the wall on the side. Somewhere into what seemed like the third hour of his speech the deacon started talking about sins. This is not verbatim but it is how I remember what he said: "Please Jesus, forgive Photini for her sins—not just the sins she actually committed but also the sins she thought about committing but never got around to. And Jesus, please forgive Photini for the sins she's committing now that she's dead." I'm sure I made that last part up but that was what it sounded like to me.

My brother was beside me on my left. He turned and said to me, "What sins? That's my mother. I'm gonna kill this guy."

I said, "Mike, killing the deacon at our mother's funeral would be hilarious and would immediately transform you into the most revered person in the family but it is probably one of those ideas that is better in theory than in application." Just then the deacon abruptly stopped yapping. He probably had another hour left in him but I think God gave him a little mini-stroke to spare our family (and possibly abort his impending homicide.)

My mother's sisters were in the front row. I don't know if you have an image in your mind of old Greek women at a funeral. I certainly do. Does the color black come to mind?

My mother's oldest sister Constance, the matriarch of the family, sent one of my cousins over to us with a message that she spoke loud enough into my ear that Larry, my wife, sister and brother could hear. "Aunty Connie says, tell Larry that his fly is open."

Larry was seated beside me on the right. He was wrecked. He and Frannie had been married fifty-one years. She went to bed, had a stroke, and was gone. Snatched away without warning—without a chance to say I love you or even goodbye. He looked like every time he exhaled he might not have the will or the strength to inhale. So I guess you could say that there was a mountain of pressure on Larry—that galaxies of pressure were pushing down on Fried Clam Larry.

As soon as my cousin delivered the message from the matriarch I saw a tiny flash of light in his eye. It wasn't even big enough to qualify as a twinkle. It was like half a twinkle. I guess you'd call it a twink. It existed for a millisecond but I saw it and I recognized it. And I knew that something was going to come out of his mouth that would be memorable. Then, Larry White from Wyman Street said, loud enough for his children to hear, a sentence that has become the stuff of legend in this family.

"You tell Aunty Connie that what can't get up can't get out."

*****

Let's set the scene for the delivery of Larry White's legendary line so that we can go beneath the surface story and attempt to appreciate it on a wider/deeper level.

I don't know where losing one's mother is on the scale of most difficult things a person has to endure in life but it's got to be near the top. At the hospital (you know, the one that greed and corruption subsequently closed), when we learned that my mother was dead I walked outside to a lovely prayer garden and I cried from the center of my solar plexus. I was convulsing and wailing and I couldn't stop. I had no control, no ability to slow down or influence in any way this oceanic wave of grief that had washed over me.

In the moments after the almighty had intervened and gently smote the tongue of the deacon and saved my brother from a homicide charge, the funeral parlor was silent.

In the previous hours all of us were distracted from the magnitude of the situation by seeing friends and loved ones who had come to pay their respects. But now it was becoming real. Our mother was going from this building to Pine Grove Cemetery in a matter of minutes. No more laughs, no more hugs, no more nothing.

You could feel the reality of the situation building in the room and inside everyone. The impending moment of *forever goodbye* had taken over and was building. It was a pressure cooker.

Larry White, the man who had his soulmate of fifty-one years snatched away, the man for whom the world as he had known it for two-thirds of his life was never going to be the same, the man who knew that he was going to live till he died without companionship, chose to burst the pressure of his family's most difficult moment … with a dick joke.

The results were immediate. Everyone in the family who heard it burst into laughter. You know when you laugh so hard that you slide off the chair? That's what happened. My dad had taken a pin to the balloon of our collective grief and it was flying around the room squealing out all of the built-up pressure.

At first people outside the immediate family were confused and concerned. It was hard for them to tell what was happening. It probably looked and sounded like hysterical grief. When they learned that it was hysterical laughter created by a perfectly timed and delivered dick joke at the most solemn of moments at our mother's funeral, they were shocked and disappointed. On behalf of my family I'd like to say that we're all sorry. We're sorry that your family has not mastered the survival skill of using humor to release tension. It must be a very hard life for you. And for those inside the family who have a twinge of residual guilt in knowing that there were people at that funeral who to this day believe that we were being disrespectful to our beloved mother, let me reiterate this powerful world view from the late great Fried Clam Larry.

Be yourself. Let them deal with it.

Aftermath

After confronting Larry about his drinking the next month of my life was a multicolored blur—it exists in my memory like a Jackson Pollock painting viewed through an unfocused lens. A steady stream of unfelt memories queued up somewhere behind my eyes and one by one, with their accompanying emotions reattached, they each took their long-awaited turn to be fully experienced. What followed was a month of me sleepwalking through life in a barely functioning haze interspersed periodically with blubbering emotional breakdowns.

I felt like such an idiot. Every time I had to pull my car over because I was being kicked in the stomach by some unleashed memory from my childhood that I was now required to feel as if it had just happened, I wanted to punch myself in the face.

I didn't have to be going through this. I was doing just fine with all this crap neatly tucked away down there. I was holding a job. I was paying my bills. I was functioning as a reasonably effective member of society. My past never bothered me. I didn't even know this stuff was in there. But now, because I'm so clueless, everything was in jeopardy. I had no way of knowing if or when this onslaught would subside. It seemed to me that the way my life was unfolding at that moment would be the way it would stay. And I could think of no examples where being a permanent emotional wreck had ever been conducive to the maintaining of gainful employment. I knew that a grown man bursting into tears every day over some shit that happened twenty years ago was always going to be the least likely candidate for employee of the month.

I saw the situation as a completely unnecessary, self-inflicted potential dismantling of my world. And with that came the weight of the following.

Within walking distance of my house there are people whose parents were murdered, whose parents were heroin addicts, who were molested as children by clergy or family members that were supposed to love and watch out for them. I was coming apart at the seams surrounded by people who would give anything to trade childhoods with me. I knew this. I still know it. But knowing that my childhood problems would be a highly desired alternative to the experiences of others (not faraway others, or theoretical others but right outside my kitchen window others) was not enough to stop my blubbering and it absolutely infuriated me. My intellect had no power over my emotions and I hated it.

Time Is Like a Baggage Handler at Newark Airport

My favorite state in the USA is New Jersey. That's not something you hear often from someone who isn't a native of the garden state. When I see New Jersey on my travel schedule I get all giddy. It's not the rural western part of that great state that is the object of my affection. I love Newark, Hoboken, and the not New York side of the Holland Tunnel because that's where the

Jersey attitude is strongest. I love the way people from eastern New Jersey navigate their world.

One time my luggage got misplaced at Newark airport. I walked up to a woman with an identification tag around her neck. I told her that my luggage didn't come out on the belt. She stared at me with a look that clearly said, "Thirty minutes and my shift will be over and here comes this sorry motherfucker." I immediately got a warm feeling because I knew that I was with someone who was going to find my suitcase. I recognized it in her attitude. My mother was like that. She would make sure you knew you were a pain in the ass while she was methodically solving your problem.

My comfort with this is almost impossible for Midwesterners to grasp. They come from a part of the world where politeness accompanies almost everything. Being from Boston, it took me a long time to get used to the Midwest. They're too friendly. It made me nervous. Here's how I explain the difference between the kind of friendly you find in the Northeast and the kind you find in the middle of the country.

If my car goes into a ditch on a snowy night in the heartland, a chatty, friendly, well-mannered local resident will stop and pull me out of the ditch. The exact same thing will happen in the Northeast except for the chatty, well-mannered parts. When a New Jersey or a Boston or a Brooklyn guy pulls you out of the ditch he does not want to hear about your family. "I saved your life. That should be enough. Now stop talking. Go away. I ain't your buddy."

So my new best friend at the airport walked me over to a staging area and found my suitcase. She didn't ask me anything about myself. She didn't engage me in any way. She got the job done in a way that was steady and completely unaffected by anything good or bad that was coming from me or anyone else.

I know that this is a minority view but I am most at ease when I am around people who get things done in a no-nonsense way. If you are trapped inside a car that is on fire the best thing you can hope for is to be in New Jersey because in all likelihood a local resident will pull you out, call you an idiot for driving a crappy car and drive away.

Steady. Reliable. Unattached. Solid … just like time.

*****

No thing that has ever been done, no thought that has ever been thought, no stress or dread that has ever been felt by any human being who ever lived has had a measurable effect on time.

The sun comes up. The sun goes down. The planet tilts a bit while it rotates. That's it. When I emerge from a period of confusion or anxiety I am comforted to know that while I was gone time clicked off every second with precision so that I could return to a world that has at least one thing in it that has never wavered—a thing completely unalterable by human thought or action. If you asked time how it felt about the human condition it wouldn't respond because it doesn't give a shit. Time heals all wounds because it is smart enough to not let any temporary life form distract it from doing its job.

When my old memories reappeared for the second, third, and fourth time I began to notice that their power over me was being slowly and steadily diminished by my new best friend … time.

It was deeply gratifying to observe time's methodical emasculation of those memories' ability to upend my world. Each precise click of each second pulled power from them. Their ability to throw my life into a tailspin was significantly diminished daily. After two months they had become powerless. Their strength had been derived entirely from having never been felt.

190 The Hitchhiking Years and Four Other Stories

The combination of my long-delayed feeling of their respective associated emotions with the steady reliable passing of time was the death knell of their power over me.

When their impotence became obvious I started taunting them. "Not so tough as you used to be are you? You're all just a bunch of freshly neutered holograms who still think you're scary. I can put my hand right through you. There's nothing there. So go away now little boys. I ain't scared and I *definitely* ain't your buddy."

The wall between these feelings and me was essential to my survival when I was a boy. It was an emergency construction built during a crisis. The builders did an excellent job. When it was finished they patted each other on the back and went home. The problem as I see it now is that I only needed to be separated from feeling this stuff until enough time had gone by for it to lose its lethal power over me. The work order for the job didn't state that the builders were to return in ten years and knock it down so I could safely feel everything and move on with my life. They built a permanent impenetrable wall to protect me from a problem that only had a ten-year life expectancy.

The wall that saves your life in a crisis winds up thwarting your growth if left in place beyond its usefulness.

I have no way of knowing how much influence these undealt-with issues had on my life prior to forcing them into the light. But I can tell you what happened in the years that followed. Right away I felt stronger in my ability to trust my decision making. I felt that there were no secret agents working against my best interests behind the scenes and that the person I wanted to be was now free to develop unhindered by the unresolved.

I was born on the day when there were finally no more unfelt traumas.

The Conversation of Old Lovers

After the last Christmas gathering at our house was over my wife and I sat quietly in the living room of our modest home. She was icing her knee. Not the knee she had replaced in July but the one she hopes to have replaced before she retires. Her hair is mostly gray now. There are a few long streaks of the raven black of her youth mixed in wistfully as a fading reminder of the journey that brought that stunning teenage adventurer to this interesting moment in time.

We talked. It was the kind of conversation that is only possible between old lovers.

After my mother died I remember trying to comprehend the magnitude of my father's loss. I couldn't. The task could not have been further beyond my capabilities. They had been married fifty-one years. They were from the same neighborhood. The depths of multilayered minutiae they had with each other were incalculable.

I did however zero in on one thing that I felt I understood enough to speculate on.

When you have built a life, raised a family, and grown from child to adult with another human who was raised in your neighborhood, the rest of the world can only guess at how all that history influences the quality of your conversations. Theresa and I can communicate more in a split second of eye contact than couples who have been married a paltry twenty years can in an hour. These double-decade-ers will often finish each other's sentences. We think that's cute. I can tell that Mrs. White knows what I'm going to say by the look on her face. I don't say it. I don't even bother to send it to her telepathically. What's the point? She already knows it. Then she will answer the thing I didn't say with a response that isn't spoken. We can continue this way for hours.

Any young person observing this will think we're sick of each other. Perhaps upon occasion we are. But that's a separate issue. We are actually practicing the deep silent communication of old lovers. It's like an energy conservation program.

As a person who treasures thoughtful conversation and its myriad possibilities, the depth of the loneliness in my father's eyes after my mother died spoke volumes to me about what was now lost forever to him.

The value of having multiple decades of intimate history with your partner cannot fully be gauged until it is gone. Theresa and I know this and we try our best to drink as deeply as possible from the well of our good fortune when and while we can.

"Don, I love the way this house feels right now."

"Me too. You know, sitting here I can almost see the laughter from the past six hours lingering near the ceiling lights. I think the walls in a home are absorbent. Tomorrow morning all this lingering laughter and love will be a permanent part of this place."

"Oh Jesus, are you gonna get all Ram Dass on me now?" And then while affecting a holier than thou tone, she said, "In the spiritual teachings it is written that if you do enough LSD the walls of the temple will reveal the history of all the enlightened souls who ever lived between them."

"You think you're funny don't ya? You know Ram Dass just died."

"Well, I guess he won't be able to *be here now*. Too soon? Yeah … probably too soon."

"Seriously though, when I was installing alarms in people's houses there were homes I went into where the silence felt toxic. I sometimes felt that if I laughed, I would be the first person to ever do so in that space."

"I was just messing with ya Donnie. Of course I know what

you mean. Silence is a complex thing. A few minutes ago while we were just sitting here I was appreciating how beautiful the silence was. Of course, then you started talking and ruined it.

"I'm kidding.

"We both know the difference between the sweet quiet of a happy home and the brutal quiet of an unhappy one. After my parents would have a big fight the thing I remember most is the icy silence that followed—sometimes for days. I remember thinking that silence should be an opportunity for a kid to feel safe and daydream about sunshiny kid stuff not an unleashing of worry and feelings of not being able to make things better. I never forgot how it felt and I'm so happy that we were able to create a home where quiet is good."

"Yeah, this house has had a ton of laughter in it. I wonder how the young couple will react when they're spending their first night in this house fifty years from now and they realize that all the walls are filled with laughter?"

"I'm sure they'll think the place is haunted."

"Right. Maybe we should leave them a note saying that we couldn't afford fiberglass to insulate the walls so we just filled 'em up with a bunch of guffaws we had hanging around."

"Nice try Donnie, I'm going to bed. Get some sleep. You'll be funnier in the morning."

"Namaste Bodhisattva."

"Namaste Shithead."

The end.

Epilogue: Larry Gets the Last Word

Don White's abbreviated summary on the parenting experience:

Have some kids. Raise 'em up. Work your ass off while doing so. Push the little buggers out into the world. Hope they make it. Hope they give you grandkids you can spoil. Try to enjoy life a bit before you die.

Did I miss anything?

In the 1990s I was working forty to sixty hours a week installing alarm systems in houses for a living. It was not uncommon for me to leave for work at 7:00 in the morning all perky and full of workingman vigor and to return home at midnight an empty vessel drained of life force and the will to live by seventeen hours of manual labor in a life of quiet desperation.

When I was fortunate enough to only work an eight-hour day, I would come home, take a shower and grab a sandwich to eat in the car as I drove back through Boston traffic to attend an open mike. I would sign up, sing two songs, drive home, pull blankets over my head around 1:00 AM, get up for work at 6:00 and do it all again. The entire decade exists in memories permanently blurred by sleep deprivation.

At this time my parents had successfully dispatched (some might say catapulted) all their children out into the world. They had been living together without chaperones or referees for a couple of years. It was a time when my siblings and I were gradually relinquishing our well-founded fear that, if left unsupervised, our parents would kill each other.

We all took turns checking in on them.

One summer afternoon in 1998 I had stopped by on my way home from work. Mom was out shopping and Larry and I were, as he would say in his signature colloquiality, "shooting the shit." It started out with the playful repartee that is the norm in our family. We were going back and forth gently teasing each other in that effortless way that is so common among working-class folks in this part of the world.

I was ribbing him about his parenting style. I forget exactly what I said, but it was about growing up with him as a hard drinker. I thought I was within the realm of this friendly teasing thing that we all do but I wasn't. It pissed him off. He gave me this look … I wish you were here because I could channel him and show it to you. I wish I were a better writer and I could describe it so well that it would jump off this page and create a visual in your mind. But you're not here and I'm not that good a writer.

What I can do is describe what happened to me the instant I saw the look on his face. It put a chill through my whole body. I knew I had crossed the line and that I was doomed. He was going to educate me in a surgical manner utilizing all the information he had gathered and stored in his back pocket database from forty years of studying my weaknesses. If that look could talk it would have said, "Your ass is mine." I was like a pantomime stuck behind an imaginary plate of glass. I couldn't escape.

He said to me, "Did you have a bike when you were a kid? I said, "You know I had a bike. You bought it for me."

"Did you ride around the town on your bike with your friends?"

"Yes, as a matter of fact I did."

"I'm happy for you. I always wanted a bike when I was a kid and I would see my friends riding around laughing and having a ball. But my father left us when I was thirteen years old and I was the oldest so I had to go to work at four in the morning at Sabanty's Bakery before school and then again after school. But you didn't have to be the breadwinner for your family at thirteen and you had a bike to ride around on with your friends. I'm happy for you."

I said, "Okay…?"

Then he said, "Have you ever been cold?"

I said, "I see what you're doing."

He raised the sound of his voice by about twenty percent. It was well below yelling volume but decidedly more authoritative. And in the voice of a man who knows he is stronger and smarter than you and is in complete control of the situation he asked the question again pausing slightly between every syllable. "Have—you—e—ver—been—cold?"

At the beginning of what I now knew was going to be a master class in how to make sure someone thinks twice about what they say before they talk to you in the future, I stood five foot eight inches tall. I had just been surgically whittled down to the size of a Ken doll. I had previously been sitting at the kitchen table but now I was standing on the chair with my eyes watching Larry from just above the tabletop.

I said, in my new squeaky doll voice, "No Dad, I've never been cold."

He said, "I was cold. My mother used to put the Jell-o next to my bed at night because it was colder in my bedroom than it was in the icebox. Now that I think about it, there has always been oil in the furnace and the radiators in this house have always been warm and you've never been cold a day in your life … *and* you had a bicycle to ride around on with your friends. I am *so* happy for you."

The words coming out of his mouth were visible to me. I could see a clear liquid dripping off of each letter. I surmised that prior to being spoken they had all been soaked in sarcasm.

The sun had gone down. The kitchen was getting dark when he walked past me and opened the refrigerator. The light silhouetted his big head making him look like a brickyard religious icon. He said, "Have you ever been hungry?"

To which I squeaked my reply, "No Dad, I've never been hungry."

"You know, thinking back on it, I believe that this refrigerator has been full of food since the day you were born. I was hungry. We ate mayonnaise sandwiches for days. My mother used to use the same tea bag for ten cups of tea. But you ...

"Never hungry,

"Never cold,

"*And* you had a bicycle to ride around on with your friends. I—am—so—hap—py—for—*you*."

At this point I was the size of a mouse. He turned around to face me. He had a package of ham and a package of cheese in his hand. During these few seconds while I was waiting for him to finish me off I was thinking about how smart he was. If he had yelled at me and called me an asshole for what I said, I could have defended myself. When someone yells at me I naturally get into a defensive position. I'm not defending myself against the point they are trying to make. I'm defending myself against being yelled at. That's why yelling at someone is an ineffective method for changing the way that person thinks. Whatever point you are trying to make goes out the window the minute you yell. The recipient is only thinking this: Stop yelling at me.

But LaLa was too smart for that. He never put me into a situation where I had any tools to defend myself. He didn't yell. He didn't call me any of the names that I'm sure he was thinking of. Instead he asked me three questions about my childhood and counterpointed them ... strategically exploiting my weaknesses and keeping me off balance. I was on the receiving end of a master class on how to utilize decades of accrued data combined with street smarts and sarcasm to completely dismantle the defenses of one's opponent without breaking a sweat. It was a thing of beauty.

For the finale of this performance he leaned toward me till

his face was ten inches from mine and said, "Look, you can say whatever you want about me and how I raised you. I'm a full-grown man. I've seen and heard everything. I'm going to love you no matter what you say or think about me. But you need to know something, and I can't believe that you're forty years old and I have to explain this to you but I am going to do it.

"When I was a kid this life that you had ...

"Never hungry,

"Never cold,

"Able to have the toys you wanted—to ride around with your friends—to not have to go to work at thirteen years old and not stop working till you retire in your sixties ... not only did I not have any of this, but I'm telling you the truth now, I didn't know it was possible. I wouldn't have been able to *dream* of this life that you're criticizing me for giving you."

He took the packages of ham and cheese and dropped them on the table in front of me for dramatic effect and said, "You look hungry. Make a sandwich." Then he walked into the living room, sat in his recliner with a big grin on his face thinking to himself, "Now that's how you do that."

On the ride home I thought about what had just happened. I thought about how much we are all shaped by what we experience when we are young—how those moments find their way into the fabric of our personalities before the cement is hardened—how much jackhammering it takes to dislodge the negative and counterproductive parts once they are identified in adulthood. I thought about kindness and empathy and generosity of spirit—how every person I ever thought was beautiful had these qualities and the closer those qualities were to the core of a person the more beautiful that person became to me. I thought that if I were a painter of portraits I would look for subjects who had kindness at their epicenter and try not to focus on their physical attributes but see if it was possible to capture the beauty of their heart.

I pulled into my driveway and turned off the engine.

Forty-year-old Don White was asking himself a question.

"Would you trade childhoods with your parents?"

If your parents had a good childhood but became drug abusers and were not able to give you the same love they received in their youth then the answer would be yes.

But for me, the answer is an unequivocal "no." So maybe it's time to quit complaining about how they raised me and get in line, like most of my ancestors did, and do the work it takes to move it forward and try to make it a little bit better for the next group coming along.

The real end.

ZEN MASTER PROLETARIAN

The Ride to Work

"You know that guy at the bar who is always snorting coke in the men's room?"

"You mean Nostril-damus?"

"Right, the guy who thinks he's predicting the end of the world for mankind, but turns out he's only predicting the end of his own stupid world."

"What about him?"

"Well, he had a doctor's appointment last week and when his doctor looked up his nose he said, 'Nostrildamus, did you lose a Camaro? Wait a minute, there's also a house, a family, some dignity and a ton of self-respect up here too.' —Whoa, whoa, slow down, stop! Let her cross. I want to enjoy her for an extra minute if it's not too much trouble sire. Ah yes, dear gentlewoman, never shall ye know the pleasure thy countenance has bestowed upon two weary groundlings. Nor how the recollection of thy magnificent form shall provide us the strength to persevere through the slings and arrows of outrageous misfortune that lie in wait for us at the suck-ass alarm installation we are bound for in our handsome Chevrolet Chariot on this glorious day beneath the firmament. —Did you see that? She likes you. No, really, I know that look. She wants you. She's got to have you—right here, right now."

"I think you're right. She might just be the one. I know, she's wealthy, young, and beautiful but maybe, just maybe, she's secretly bored with yuppie boys and trust funders named Chip and in her quiet moments she dreams of being ravaged by a fifty-year-old balding guy with a beer gut, coffee breath, and a pair of linesman pliers in his pocket. What? Don't look at me like that. These things happen. I read it online so it's gotta be true. The world is full of beautiful buxom wealthy women longing to act out their sexual fantasies on an unsuspecting pimple-faced pizza delivery boy or an overweight mailman and I've been waiting pa-tiently for my turn to deliver my best three-minute performance to that one sweet thing who has longed all her life for a sponta-neous encounter with a middle-aged alarm installer. And I think today just might be the day."

"Three minutes?"

"Sure, if I get eight hours of sleep the night before and take my multivitamin."

"Where the hell are we going today anyway?"

"We're going to start that huge job I landed in Wellesley."

"Wellesley. You know what I love about that town? It's the way the people are so down to earth, how they're always so friendly to the people who are working in their homes, you know, offering them coffee and being genuinely interested and curious about their families and the struggles and challenges that working people have. —Oh … Wait a minute. Did you say Wellesley? I thought you said Dorchester. Fuck Wellesley."

"I wasn't going to take this job, because the owner has a well-deserved reputation for being a world-class bastard. When I went to the site to scope it out, there was a guy walking around with an armful of blueprints who had been thrown off the job. He was tryna get paid for the work he had already done.

"If the owner thinks he can replace you, he'll fire you. If not, like with this poor guy, he says, 'We agreed on thirty thousand. Now that the work's done I think it's only worth fifteen.' Then when the contractor says, 'You owe me thirty thousand and that's what you're gonna pay me.' The owner says, 'Here's a check for fifteen you can take it or leave it. But if you take me to court I'll make sure it costs you sixty thousand in lawyer's fees.'

"I'm only doing this job because the electrical contractor begged me to do it and promised that he would pay me directly and that I wouldn't have to be another guy walking around the mansion at the end of the project with my tail between my legs hoping to get fifty percent of my money."

"Is the guy really that rich?"

"Look, you and I have been doing this work now for what … twenty years? And we think we've met rich people before. But this guy is in a category all by himself. Let me give you some perspective. Wellesley is populated with some of the richest people in the country. Most of the people in this town have lived their whole lives getting exactly what they want, exactly when and exactly how they want it. Nobody ever tells these people that they can't do anything—ever.

"Just think about that for a few minutes. Here's a town with, let's say, ten thousand extremely wealthy people living in it who for generations have been accustomed to getting the whole rest of the world to jump as soon as they snap their fingers. As far as I can see there isn't one of these sonsabitches who was ever told that he wasn't permitted to do something who couldn't get that decision reversed in twenty minutes with one phone call.

"Then some guy buys a huge chunk of land in their precious

hamlet and tells (not asks) the town that he is going to divide it up into parcels. The town, of course, tells him that is not allowed in Swellesley—there are ordinances that say it's wetlands or conservation land or was once owned by President Kennedy. Then they walk away congratulating themselves on how well their lawyers have protected their town from development only to wake up a week later to see that the guy has done just what he said he would do and the land is all subdivided.

"Then (you'll love this) the guy says, 'And oh, by the way, I'm putting in a helicopter landing pad on my newly divided chunk of land so I can fly in and out whenever I damn well please.' At which time the town full of people living under the delusion that they are as rich and powerful as our new employer say, 'Oh no you will not!' and they convene a town meeting to show him who's boss.

"So with the town hall parking lot filled with the most expensive cars in the world and the inside of the building filled with impending victory because there is a zillion dollars' worth of money, power, and always-getting-your-way assembled there to put this new out-of-towner in his place, they hold their meeting. But he doesn't show up because he's in England signing a gajillion dollar deal with the British government and he can't be bothered with these insects. Instead he sends one of his army of lawyers, who talks for five minutes and walks out leaving behind a room full of freshly neutered rich people.

"What did this lawyer say you ask? He said, 'My client has unlimited resources. Un-li-mi-ted. If you fuck with him he will sue the town of Wellesley and keep it tied up in court until the legal fees completely bankrupt the place.' Then he walked out and sure as shit a year from now the town fathers will be looking out the window of what they thought were mansions and watching his helicopter take off from the one real mansion in town."

The Graying of Black and White

An observant alarm installer often has a view into the real world of the people for whom he is working that reveals a tremendous amount of information about who they really are—information that people often go to great lengths to conceal.

It takes anywhere from four to twenty hours to install a complete security system in a house. So for over twenty years now Dennis and I have spent a great deal of time in the homes of people who come from all sorts of economic, ethnic, religious, and political backgrounds. And because we are in every room in their house installing security devices on all their windows and doors for such a long time our customers eventually forget we are there and just go about their lives leaving a window open for us to look through—a window into who and how they are when no one is watching.

So for two decades now while we have been screwing security switches into the windows of America we have simultaneously been getting schooled in the intimate ways in which people behave in the comfort of their own homes. (People with whom we often have nothing in common but the desire to keep the type of characters which Dennis and I would have a much greater chance of knowing personally from burglarizing their premises.)

It's a little like being invisible.

We see how they treat their kids, how they talk on the phone, what they say about the person they just talked to after they hang up, and countless other everyday things that they participate in or navigate through in their regular lives.

Over time this constant exposure to people outside our circle chips away at and eventually dismantles each and every stereotype that a working-class guy would have unwittingly embraced from a childhood shaped by friends and family of a specific worldview.

I have worked for rich people who were warm and wonderful as well as rich people who demanded I buy them a new house because I left a dirty fingerprint on their wallpaper. I have worked for poor people who were generous and caring to a fault as well as poor people who were so rude, crude, and dishonest that I have on several occasions contemplated putting my screwdriver across the power terminals to fry their alarm panel and thereby expedite my departure from their company.

Knowledge has a way of consuming the oxygen that stereotypes need to continue breathing. It creates those annoying gray areas that cloud up the black and white world that existed so comfortably in our minds before indisputable facts came in and screwed everything up. It educates us on how to get along with a wide cross section of people from worlds other than our own.

*****

I grew up in an urban working-class family. Both of my parents worked in factories. They were members of unions. They were Democrats. They voted for anyone named Kennedy when possible and for any generic Democrat when not. I don't recall having ever been in the company of a self-proclaimed Republican until I left home for the first time. In fact, I believe I could have argued that there was no such thing—that they didn't exist.

However, once I did leave my union factory town I quickly learned that not only do they exist but that entire swaths of the country are totally and irretrievably overrun with them.

Begin Digression.

In the early 1990s I spent a week camping out at a folk festival in Texas. The level of my unpreparedness for this event was astounding. I had some money, a toothbrush, and a guitar. The guy I drove with had a twenty-dollar tent that we set up at night and within which we were nearly baked alive by an ornery sun that turned our rudimentary domicile into a fully functioning pizza oven by 9:00 AM.

We were hopelessly outmatched by the deadly combination of an unforgiving environment and our lack of knowledge and respect for it.

I didn't know that the sun was a lethal weapon. I'm from New England. Our sun is friendly. My car didn't even have air conditioning.

The murderous sun, we soon learned, was not a solitary assassin. It was merely the first in a relentless series of Texan environmental assaults designed specifically, it seemed, to punish first-time visitors who naively assumed that they could visit the Lone Star State without the benefit of due diligence.

How could I have known, for example, that these miserable little things called chiggers would bite you in the ball sack if you sat on the grass without a blanket? Really, Texas? You can't sit on the grass here without getting your junk chewed by bugs?

Anyway, before noon we were adopted by an extended family who shared some of their shade with us so the inside of our tent wouldn't broil during the day. They told me I should drink lots of this stuff called . . . water? And when I didn't, they brought me back from death by stupidity by feeding me salted peanuts.

We shared songs and poetry all night. They fed us. They introduced us to their friends. These people were the warmest, most caring and wonderful people I had ever met and I loved them. I loved them. I loved them.

Then five days into our New England/Texas love fest I learn that not only were they all Republicans but, sweet weeping Jesus, they were all of that special horrifying variety that not only liked and listened to right wing radio but bought all the pundit's books and would proudly quote them accurately and often.

I was instantly hurled into an emotional and intellectual crisis. I just kept walking around the campsite mumbling to myself, "You bastards! You made me love you first. Now all of my multigenerational, liberal arguments that have served me so well for all of these decades are useless to me. I can't accuse you of not caring about disadvantaged people. You have shown me, a stranger, more genuine care in my time of need than people I have known all my life. Your kindness and generosity has diabolically neutered my ability to dismiss your politics with my well-worn argument that *your* worldview is void of compassion."

And so began the inevitable graying of *my* worldview from the black-and-white-good-is-good-bad-is-bad-right-is-right-wrong-is-wrong-ness of my youth to the extremely annoying and infinitely less satisfying almost-everybody-has-at-least-a-partial-point-of-view-that-is-valid-and-important-to-be-open-to-ness of my later years.

Unapologetic partisans live in a world without complications. They never have to partake in the distasteful humanizing of persons with opposing views. "Those people are just wrong" and, by extension, inferior . . . the end. No more messy thinking required.

In a media-driven political world that thrives on contentious sound bites, humanizing the gray area in your opponent's argument is not considered an indication that you are an evolutionarily advanced being. The fact that you live in a world ruled by a subset of beings with severely underdeveloped anterior insular cortexes (the part of the brain where empathy lives) ensures that your thoughtfulness will be seen as a weakness for which you will pay dearly via an onslaught of partisan talking points guaranteeing that you and your fully developed human brain will never be invited back to the CNN roundtable of unmovable opinions.

End digression.

Zen Master Dennis

The front seat of the work van on the way to a job is a place where the secret language of our endangered species of Zen Master Proletarians is spoken. We are a rare breed Dennis and I among our brethren tradesmen. Rare because, much like the previously referenced stereotypes, as alarm installers we are exactly what you would expect us to be sixty percent of the time, exactly what you would hope we could be twenty percent of the time and something that you would never dream we could be the other twenty percent of the time.

It is the nature of stereotypes to be half accurate to justify their existence in the minds of people who are too lazy or otherwise unmotivated to acknowledge that a significant percentage of the people being casually lumped into these categories are not at all like the image being cavalierly dispensed around the water cooler.

Dennis taught me how to do this work over twenty years ago. He took me on as a helper and taught me the trade that eventually enabled me to buy a house, raise a family and stave off the lifetime of poverty that I had unwittingly designed for my life through a series of bad decisions and a visceral disdain for corporations.

In the two decades that we have worked together I have grown into a deep appreciation for the way he navigates the testosterone-saturated world in which we work with the nimble footwork of a man who is half ballet dancer and half prize fighter. It is so impressive to me that were I to be honest I would be forced to admit that the whole point of writing this story is to create a format within which I can hold the attention of a reader with an interesting story long enough to allow me to simultaneously describe the working-class genius of my friend.

I have always felt that many people confuse an education or

an ability to memorize information with intelligence. The most intelligent people I have ever met were those who could gather information quickly and accurately and then use it to make a good decision. I suppose there are a lot of overeducated people who are also capable of this type of behavior. (Disregarding, as we have recently learned to, stereotypes like that of the MIT professor who is advancing the entire world with his work in physics but needs help crossing the street because he doesn't understand that the white lines of a crosswalk don't have any inherent ability to stop a moving automobile, that they merely represent a suggestion, if you will, to the driver.) The truth as far as I can see is that the ability to gather quickly and utilize information is often done at the highest level by un- or under-educated people who live in a world where violence is prevalent and excelling at this skill is a matter of life and death.

Dennis has a profound and nuanced understanding of the way things work in his world and he uses that understanding to his advantage every day. Here's a good example; a classic actually. Years ago we worked for a security company that landed the job of installing a fire system for the home of the lead singer for a famous rock band. Subsequent to the installation there was a fire at the house. I never learned any of the details but whatever happened or didn't happen the fire system didn't work in a way that was acceptable to the homeowner and he was, as you might imagine, very upset with the company.

Everyone who had previously worked on the system was completely starstruck and anxious to be in, and later talk about being in, the home of a real rock star. Dennis was not immune to this. In fact he was and still is a big fan of the band. Unfortunately for him he was sent to the home after the damage had occurred and was therefore denied the opportunity to meet the happy rock star version of the singer. Instead, when the doorbell was answered, my friend was face to face with the furious version.

For a moment Dennis wasn't sure what was happening as the rock star voiced his outrage because, as he puts it, the guy kept yelling the name of the salesperson who had sold him the system in a manner that at first sounded like singing. So off-guard and off-balance Dennis walked past the angry minstrel, set his toolbox on the floor, and opened it in preparation of installing a temporary fire system to protect the premises while not being exactly sure of what was happening.

However, the next moment revealed that the vocalist was not serenading the alarm man but was actually taking out his perfectly understandable frustrations on the first living being he had encountered from the company. The fact that his anger sounded melodic is, I suppose, a testament to his talent.

Having discerned to the best of his ability what was transpiring Dennis immediately employed a psychological tool he had developed and used with great success in several past hostile situations.

Without engaging (which he knew would only pour accelerant on the flaming situation and pull him into an unwinnable battle) he calmly and dispassionately closed his toolbox, lifted it by the handle, and walked toward the door.

"Where are you going?" sang the angry rock star. "I'm leaving," said the calm and all inner peace-y tradesman Zen master. "What do you mean, you're leaving?" sang the rock star.

Then, like a psychiatrist who speaks with an exaggerated calm in his voice to an agitated patient Dennis said, "I had nothing to do with the selling or the installation of this system. Here are the phone numbers of the salesman and the installation manager. I am only here to make sure that your house is protected while people much more important than me decide what to do about what happened before I got here. I am very good at what I do. That's why they sent me. But it appears that you don't want me to do this work so I'm leaving. It was nice to meet you. I'm a big fan."

At this point the entire dynamic of the situation shifted. The rock star realized, what all good sages know, that the person who is not attached to money, pride, glory, or praise, is exactly the person that you want in your world. So he asked him to put his tools back down and showed him the work he wanted done.

The Hal 9000

For several weeks in the colossal basement of the richest man in the world Dennis and I had pulled thousands of feet of fire and burglary cable all terminating at an alarm panel the inside of which appeared to be fully capable of decoding the human genome while simultaneously eavesdropping on every cell phone conversation on earth.

An alarm panel's job is to detect an intrusion or fire, ring a siren, and notify the authorities. For those who want to spend more money these basic functions can happen with more pizzazz (touchpads that can talk for example) but the job description is always the same:

Detect problem.

Wake up resident.

Scare away bad guy.

Call appropriate civil servants.

The alarm panel in this house was something completely different than anything we had ever seen. As I began to learn about its capabilities I must confess to being a little creeped out by the thing. I started referring to it as Hal 9000, a reference that was lost on the younger members of the crew but described perfectly to Dennis and me its potential for becoming a sentient being and someday refusing to open the pod bay doors.

Hal could, in fact, open and close doors, water the lawn, drain the pool, fill the pool, and, as Dennis so delicately put it, "do the wife in a pinch."

There were cameras all around the house and inside of every room. They were, of course, all tied to Hal and therefore accessible via an internet connection. Once functional, the richest man in the world would be able to simultaneously observe the gardener weeding in the yard and his children watching TV from his phone while on a break from a meeting in a boardroom in China. There was a big screen on a wall in the kitchen upon which his chiseled chin could appear so that he could have some sort of futuristic, interactive, hologram breakfast experience with his family from the other side of the globe.

As good as Dennis is at alarm installation, he knew that he was over his head with this panel so he hired a technician who claimed to have experience with the Hal 9000 to do the final wiring and programming.

Dennis is meticulous about the art of wiring. When you look at the inside of a panel he wired it looks like it was done in a factory by a precision calibrated machine. All wires are stripped at exactly the same length with everything straight up and down and bent at perfect ninety-degree angles. It's just the way he is. If you could see a diagram of the inside of his brain I'm sure it would be wired like one of his panels. He can't sleep at night if a wire is two degrees to the left of perfectly straight.

The technician that he hired to wire this bad boy did not suffer from the same obsessive compulsive wiring disorder as Dennis and as a result his wiring job looked more like it had been done by a human being: neat and nice but well shy of perfect.

The Overview

The height of the cathedral ceiling in the great room is such that I must stand, against OSHA regulations, on the first rung from the top of my fourteen-foot stepladder to secure an endless line of red fire wire to the joists before the drywall crew arrives to install the ceilings. From my precarious perch I have an excellent overview of the bustling myriad of tradesmen worker bees in this palatial hive.

The inside of a mansion under construction is many things: cold or hot depending on the season, busy, dangerous, loud, dusty, dirty. I have contemplated writing in detail about all the sights and sounds of this world but I can't imagine that I would be less bored describing it than I am in my daily enduring of it. I will however devote a few paragraphs to the fact that a construction crew is, outside of most professional sports teams, one of the few exclusively male environments left in America. For those of you who have never had the pleasure of witnessing the behavior and overhearing the dialogue of working-class men when their primal maleness is unconstrained and allowed to run free my forthcoming description may provide an interesting voyeuristic window into this secret man-tribe. It may also traumatize some of you.

The first rule of survival in this world is to know what not to talk about.

My dad was a bartender. He told me a bartender never talks about politics or religion. (He also said that when you climb over the bar and hit the guy who hit the woman, the woman who got hit by the guy will break a bottle over your head for hitting the guy who hit her.) I have no way of knowing if this specific pearl of wisdom from my padre might ever find a moment for practical application in your life but I felt an obligation to include it here just in case.

You're welcome.

Back to what not to talk about. The bartender's goal is to keep his or her patrons drinking and tipping. That's why you will never see any seasoned barkeep veer too far from topics of conversation that don't provoke strong personal opinions. The list of infallibly safe subjects is short. Here it is:

Number 1: Sports

Number 2: Sports

Number 3: Sports

The difference between saying you hate the way your local hockey team played last night and saying you hate what a specific politician from a specific political party said in his speech last night is one of the important things you need to be aware of to survive on the construction site. The former can make you part of the team. The latter can ruin your life by making you a focal point.

Let's assume you are a poet with a degree in literature but because the job market for your particular skill set is, shall we say, weak, you wind up swinging a hammer to keep your mortgage paid. Announcing that you are a poet while you are sitting on a plywood floor with twelve other tradesmen at lunch is pretty much the same as announcing that you have a vagina. Sensitivity, compassion, empathy, nuance, while noble and beneficial attributes in many other parts of the world, are weaknesses here and to be the recipient of a perceived weakness in the man club is to find oneself in a very unfortunate state of affairs.

The conversation beneath my lofty perch this day is primarily about sports—specifically, the Boston Bruins. How they don't check anymore. How they let the New York Rangers rough them up all over the place—pretty safe stuff. There is also a fair amount of he-man chatter on the subject of female genitalia. Since there are no women in this testosterone factory, in addition to sports the safe list here also includes the subject of female erogenous zones (provided it is not in the context of someone accusing you of having one because you may know what a sonnet is.)

The Brazilian electrician's radio is blaring folk/pop music in Portuguese. The carpenters have the classic rock station turned up equally loud. My right ear is taking in the sounds of accordions and trumpets with a boom-cha Latin beat while my left ear is hearing "Whipping Post" by the Allman Brothers. This irreconcilable clashing of sounds causes my brain to go into a semi-dormant state within which it is able to function well enough to keep me from falling off the ladder but not with enough capacity to attempt to decode what it is hearing. Plumbers are hauling long sections of copper pipe on their shoulders. Carpenters are banging nails. Just to the right of my ladder a man is cutting long strips of wood on a table saw creating loud buzzing sounds and sawdust geysers that float gently in the air coating the inside of my lungs with each inhalation and gently settling upon every uncovered inch of the place. His proximity to my ladder creates the possibility that should I fall at just the right angle my head could be severed from my shoulders before my torso hits the floor. Every corner of this scene is alive with the movement of bodies carrying building materials and the sounds of hammers, music, power saws, and macho-man talk.

"Get your thumb outta your ass and unload those pallets." "This Bruins team sucks so bad." "The blueprints are always wrong, don't get your panties in a wad over it." "Do you think Johnny Bucyk and Derek Sanderson would have let the Rangers treat them like bitches and not hit back?" "Joey, the electrical inspector says he won't pass us unless you blow him. Go ahead kid, it's time to take one for the team." "Those Bruins teams from the seventies would have beat the shit out of those guys and then climbed into the crowd and started pounding their loudmouth fans too."

There is no moment that is not filled with disparate sounds and no corner of this place that does not contain bodies in motion. Then, without warning all the talking stops. Followed shortly by the abrupt termination of Portuguese music. Two seconds later mid guitar solo the Allman Brothers go silent. The movement of bodies continues unabated. Were it not for the hammering and the buzzing of the table saw it would be like a scene from a silent movie.

The first time I witnessed this curtailment of music and conversation I was so bewildered that I thought my brain was losing the capacity to hear voices and music and that I might be having a mini stroke. I have long since reconciled that notion with the knowledge that the one and only thing that can always silence music and conversation on a job site is the arrival of the owner.

Periphery

When you are raised in a working-class community where the primary problem-solving option is violence and the secondary one is more violence you learn early on that what you say, especially to and around people you don't know, should be respectful.

I have on more than one occasion seen a full-grown man from a suburban town visit our proletarian sanctuary, get drunk, and start running his mouth as if there were no possibility that someone would pummel his cranium until from that mouth emerged the same primal high-pitched shriek/squeal that a dog makes when a car bumper has delivered him a freshly shattered hipbone.

Our life experiences make it almost inconceivable here that

a person with a propensity for what we colloquially call "talking shit" could live past the age of twelve.

Another survival skill we acquire and develop in grade school is the ability to see without looking.

If you are going to school with or drinking in a bar alongside current or future tough guys (construction workers, bikers) you may have many friends but eye contact is not one of them. One of the most terrifying questions in the English language to me is: "What the hell are you looking at?"

Honestly, just typing those seven words caused my metabolism to unleash a fight or flight adrenalin blast so powerful that I had to shut off my computer and sit in the lotus position doing meditative breathing exercises for twenty minutes before my heart rate would permit me to refocus on this paragraph.

The percentage of times in my life when I have heard that question and was not subsequently witness to physical violence is small enough to be deemed statistically inconsequential.

Expertise in the use of peripheral vision here is no less of an essential ingredient to one's prospective longevity as are air, water, and nourishment.

Were you to have observed Dennis and I performing our respective duties when the Richest Man in the World made his appearance on the job site that day you would have been hard pressed to find any evidence to contradict our tacit claim that we were completely oblivious to all but the tasks before us.

The truth, as is often the case, was opposite the obvious. While Dennis was drilling holes in windowsills using one percent of his attentiveness to ensure that he didn't penetrate his own hand he was simultaneously using the remaining ninety-nine percent covertly observing every movement of this man as if his life depended on it.

Power

Bob the Electrician is bigger, stronger, and handsomer than ninety percent of all the men you have ever met and one hundred percent of all the other men on this job site.

If your women's magazine needs a cover model for a three-page spread dedicated to appreciation for the physical attributes of construction workers, Bob's your man. Just tell the modeling agency that you need a broad-shouldered, five-o'clock-shadowed, classically handsome, six-foot Adonis in his early thirties with large tattooed biceps, who drives a Harley Davidson and looks great in a hard hat and they will send him to you.

Bob's impressive upper body is often concealed beneath a sweat-soaked t-shirt with his name above the pocket and the company logo on the back. But should his highly advanced olfactory system pick up the slightest hint of female endorphins or ovulation within a mile of the job site, his shirt will tear itself off his torso and he will find a reason to justify working shirtless in the front of the building.

From inside the building the rest of us on the crew will sneak the occasional envious peek as a stream of desperate housewives meander up to Bob to ask fabricated questions about the job that apparently only he is qualified to answer. We are like the overweight friends of the twenty-year-old bikinied beauty at the beach. Our shirts are like a cotton suit of armor protecting and defending us from the terrifying possibility that one of these women might be forced to make a comparison between Bob's pectoral magnificence and our paunch and manboobs.

Within the context of physical attractiveness to the opposite sex—especially from the unfortunate perspective of men less blessed—this electrician has a ton of power. It would be reasonable to extrapolate and assume that his prowess exists equally in other arenas of his life. But even cursory investigative research would reveal the frailty of that hypothesis.

*****

The next section of this story would have fit the established theme of things-not-always-being-what-they-seem beautifully if Jordan Walsh, known formerly as the Richest Man in the World, were a short chubby bald guy. He isn't. He couldn't look more like what you'd expect if he were drawn as an evil banker for a comic book—blonde hair, blue eyes, over six feet tall, high cheekbones with a chin that is the beneficiary of a thousand years of skillful breeding.

He has a strong body. But unlike Bob's, which was created by lifting weights, Mr. Wash's frame is the taut, wiry type, common among affluent men, that is built and maintained through years of regular visits to the racquet ball court.

From twelve feet above my newly silenced workplace I watch him walk directly to Bob. What next transpires is an impressive example of how real power functions in the world.

Mr. Walsh calls Bob down from a ladder with the same words one would use to call a dog. "Come here." That's all he says and the electrician whose bicep forearm combination could crush the skull of every person he ever met immediately descends and follows him the same way that a puppy follows his owner around the house while the owner points at strewn trash and chewed shoes saying, "Did you do this?"

These two men are roughly the same height. But Jordan dwarfs Bob—not physically—a photograph wouldn't show it. It's not something you see. It's something you feel. It has nothing to do with size. It has only and everything to do with power. Real power. Jordan Walsh has REAL POWER. It screams out from the tone and inflection of every word he says—from the way each step he takes toward you proclaims his invincibility—from how the way he tilts his head makes you want to cup your ball sack—from how the way he leans into you when he talks sends a clear message to your central nervous system that were he to blow your brains out in front of all thirty people on this job site not one of them would testify against him.

On the scale of real power over which this man presides, skull-crushing biceps and the ability to generate a bit of moisture in the loins of bored housewives is laughably insignificant and probably unworthy of even footnote recognition.

This power is filtered down to the world through its ownership of multilayered offshore tax shelters disguised as corporations by the most expensive lawyers in the world. This power is absolute. Governments tremble in its presence. Nation States do its bidding. Your eyes don't see it. They don't need to. The ancient part of you that releases the adrenaline explosion when you are being attacked by a tiger sees it, feels it, knows it, and immediately commands you into a submissive posture. The evolutionary metabolic biology that has sustained your species for two hundred thousand years recognizes that survival in the face of this alpha force is possible only through its benevolence.

Bob and his crew had spent weeks running electrical cable and mounting back boxes for seventy-five ceiling lights throughout the building. Each was installed precisely as specified by the blueprints.

From the top of my ladder I watched without looking as Mr. Walsh (figuratively) pulled Bob around the job site by the ear pointing at back box locations and commanding that each one be moved seven inches to the left to line up with the center of the corresponding window.

In the absence of absolute power this scene would have played out like a thousand before it that I have seen. It is perhaps the most common and predictable interaction that occurs between owner and contractor. The owner says he doesn't like the way the work looks. The contractor says, "That's a shame, but I'm not a mind reader. I did the work per the prints that *you* provided me." Then he details how many man-hours it will take to undo and then redo the work attaching a dollar figure to the estimate that includes a hidden "aggravation fee." They haggle over the price, come to an uncomfortable agreement and life goes on.

Bob spoke not a single word. He made notes on a clipboard. He didn't argue, contest or state the obvious. His silence acknowledged the reality of the situation and how its dearth of viable options forced him to reconcile himself to complete subservience.

Real power tornados the human beings in its path with the same consideration that one gives an ant whose route home has brought him underfoot. No one is more acutely aware of the complete insignificance of all life forms beneath the shoe of real power than a man whose power is exaggerated by the masses.

Later Bob will drive his motorcycle to a secluded wooded area, review the day in his mind while doing math alongside his clipboard notes. The numbers will prove what he had already surmised—that the extra work will consume sixty percent of the profit and that in five weeks he will have completed three months of ten-hour days and have less money to show for it than if he had been working at a job that paid the minimum wage.

Bob's unfortunate fiscal reality was not caused by mistakes he or his crew made or by underbidding the job and failing to anticipate the actual costs or for any reason attributable to anything of his own doing. Bob the electrician is going to perform three months of skilled, licensed, hard labor for the minimum wage because, and only because, real power waved its hand and proclaimed that it would be so.

The First Confrontation

I'm getting too old for this work.

Construction is a young man's game. Twenty-five years of swinging hammers, lifting heavy objects, working in sub-zero temperatures and breathing sawdust will guarantee that throughout your golden years your vocabulary will be periodically augmented by your family physician with terms like Shoulder Arthroscopy, Uncompartmental Knee Replacement, Torn Meniscus, and Reactive Airway Disease.

I am the oldest guy on the crew. At the end of a ten-hour day all the parts of my body where one bone connects to another are begging for anti-inflammatory drugs and cursing me for not studying harder in school.

Young men work all day, party all night then work all day again thinking primarily of women. The oldest man on the crew works all day, sleeps all night, works all day again wincing, mumbling, and thinking primarily about inevitable shoulder surgery.

We had stacked our unused wire in a corner of the electrical room and were about to call it a day when Mister Jordan Walsh loped into the room with the general contractor in tow.

I stood in the doorway and watched as Jordan began a verbal assault on Dennis. Initially it was about the Hal 9000—the way it was wired. In the opinion of the only person whose opinion mattered, the wiring was messy and completely unacceptable. He informed Dennis that it would be rewired. It wasn't an order. Orders, at least in theory, can be disobeyed. It was an edict. It was law.

Before Dennis could defend himself the assault turned to the subject of smoke detectors. Jordan had purchased thirty-five of them and decreed that these would be the ones that would be installed. Earlier in the week Dennis, through multiple diplomatic channels, had sent a message to the Emperor stating that he would not install equipment that he did not purchase himself for the same reason he had refused to do so for every other person he had ever worked for: "I am obligated to service this system. Every time there is a problem or a false alarm I have to fix it. I only use UL listed devices that will not false alarm. I will not install any equipment that virtually ensures that I will be climbing out of bed to drive to Wellesley every time someone burns a piece of toast."

The insolence of this insurgent proclamation laid the groundwork for the epic confrontation between these two battle-hardened strategists that was unfolding before me.

Mister Walsh was in his natural state of dominance and intimidation. Dennis was digging in and preparing to defend himself. The reiteration of his argument against using inferior equipment was interrupted momentarily by the general contractor who attempted to offer some mediation and was neutered mid-sentence when Jordan snapped, "Shut up. This has nothing to do with you." His words were accompanied by a chilling glare that communicated an encyclopedia's worth of information regarding the magnitude and versatility of the military options at his disposal.

While Jordan was leaning his torso forward saying "I know how this works. You use your parts, mark them up and I pay extra" my eyes were fixed upon the hammer in my friend's right hand.

Each word Dennis spoke seemed to make Jordan bigger and stronger. I felt like I was watching an episode of The Incredible Hulk. When Dennis said "I don't" Jordan's chest busted the buttons of his shirt. The words "ever use" engorged his calf muscles tearing his pant legs up to his knees, and the verbalizing of these seven syllables "inferior equipment" poured so much accelerant onto the furnace of Jordan's fury that to my delirious eye he turned green and burst out of his clothes.

As I was reminding myself that this was not a cartoon and that it was in my interest to keep my mind attuned to what was actually happening I was observing how the fingers on Dennis's right hand were gripping and releasing the hammer handle. It was exactly the same way a major league hitter grips a Louisville Slugger while awaiting a full count fastball. It is a movement that says, "I am intensely focused *and* relaxed. And at the right time every muscle in my body will work together toward the singular goal of crushing the ball."

As the situation intensified Dennis saw his options begin to disappear. The pack-up-my-tools-and-leave trick wasn't going to work here. And it was obvious that subsequent perpetual interruptions of Dennis's sleep patterns were of no concern to Mister Walsh.

When a person is in a life-or-death situation the speed with which detailed information can be accessed and analyzed is impressive. In a split second Dennis considered and rejected dozens of options from his database of previous experience, while simultaneously observing every movement of the person before him and the two in his periphery.

In the midst of a situation that was rapidly coming to a boil a voice in his mind was talking. "If I hit this guy, which is something I REALLY want to do, my life as I have known it will be over. I'll lose my house and my business. Everything I have worked my ass off for twenty-five years will disappear.

"The choices here are clear. Let this guy screw me or lose everything."

No one with a family to support and a business that took a quarter of a century to build can man up under this kind of pressure. Jordan knows this so well that he never has to think about it. Acquiescence via the threat of overwhelming force is the cornerstone of all his business dealings.

However, leaning against the doorframe with the scene before me I knew that in all of Jordan Walsh's past business dealings it was unlikely that he had ever encountered an opponent whose life experience imbued into the fiber of his being a deeper hatred of bullies combined with a temper so hot that it could shut off the oxygen to the parts of his brain where rational decision making resides.

I saw the look in my friend's eye at the exact moment when he was saying to himself, "I may just have to kill this motherfucker."

Dennis's face turned bright red. His eyes glazed over and the fingers on his right hand stopped flexing and were holding the hammer handle so tightly that I thought I saw a drop of sap squeeze out of it.

"Lose everything or bend over? Those are my choices? Fuck it. If he comes one inch closer to me I am going to reach back and swing this hammer from the back of my kneecaps with every ounce of force and follow-through this body can muster. If this next moment is going to destroy my world, I'm going to get my money's worth out of it. He may be able to ruin my life but he will not live to gloat about it."

Jordan had imperceptibly inched to within two feet of Dennis and was leaning his head forward in what was an obvious posture of dominance. From Dennis's perspective, however, it was a very generous way of lowering his noggin into the sweet spot where Dennis could bring the full force of his career-ending homerun swing down upon it without having to stand on his toes to do so.

At what seemed to be the exact moment where the pressure of the situation could no longer be contained, I saw the general contractor give Dennis a look that existed in the world for half of the time it would take to wink.

Although Dennis was intensely focused on every movement of the person before him, his acute adrenaline-driven sensory perception also extended to his peripheral vision and without shifting his gaze from Jordan he saw and fully understood everything that was communicated in the contractor's fleeting glance.

In the secret facial language that workers, butlers, maids, and virtually everyone who works under oppression speak fluently, the contractor had told Dennis that he would make this right with him—that he would make sure that he got paid for the extra work and that he wouldn't have to service the fire system.

I heard the hissing of steam being released from heat pipes. Dennis loosened his death grip on the hammer. His body relaxed. The rage left his eyes. And he said, "Okay. I'll rewire the panel and I'll use your smokes."

The Father

"I must say that I am impressed with the fact that we got through this job without you having an aneurysm or killing anyone."

It was Christmas Eve. Dennis had just navigated the winding quarter-mile driveway to the mansion. He threw the shifter into park and said, "You don't know the half of it. Four days ago the GC forced me to come here for an electrical inspection that both of us knew was not going to happen. It didn't matter that no inspectors have ever worked on Christmas week—unless if by working you mean get drunk while still on the clock at the first bar within walking distance of the inspection office.

"I told the GC 'Don't waste my time and take me away from my family' but, as we have come to know during our months of indentured servitude on this job, making workers jump through hoops and not paying them for it is what makes life worth living for the person who owns the palace you see before you. And since I had yet to get paid I went, waited two hours for the no one that we all knew wasn't coming, recited my mantra to keep my head from exploding and drove an hour home.

"Believe me, if the owner or the GC had shown up I'd be looking at twenty to life and you'd be dropping these prints off tonight by yourself."

It was dark now. Dennis took a folder with blueprints and assorted final paperwork from the dashboard and went inside. The plan was to leave it for the owner and to make sure there were no loose ends that needed to be tied up before we put this job behind us.

I was waiting in the van when out of the darkness one of the workers on the painting crew appeared at the passenger window and began talking to me about the owner and the job. It was a predictable small talk conversation between proletarians indistinguishable in my mind from thousands before, except that he kept hinting that there was more to this situation than the owner being powerful and difficult to work for—that there was a back story worth knowing. I prodded him for details and immediately became aware of the plausible deniability that his lack of forthrightness was protecting and acknowledged it by curtailing my inquiries. Just before he walked back into the darkness he said, "Google him."

While I was waiting for Dennis to return, I took my phone out of my pocket and asked the internet what it knew about a Mister Jordan Walsh. The internet dutifully delivered me a ten-year-old Los Angeles Times story.

Jordan Walsh, it began, had a twin brother named Jonathan. The family lived in Southern California where their father was an extremely powerful state senator.

I have been in the company of many bad guys in my life. They are always interesting. Not because they are bad, but because they are complex. It is the possibility of glimpsing a well-concealed particle of goodness in a bad guy that make him worthy of my time and intellectual investment. It is with sadness and regret that I must reveal to you that my extensive research into the man who fathered the richest man in the world has uncovered no identifiable redeeming qualities.

He was by all accounts the cruelest, most corrupt, morally bankrupt politician in the golden state's storied history of such things. He was one hundred percent buyable. His support was openly for sale to the highest bidder. He had been in politics all his life. He owned the legal system from top to bottom. His bought-and-paid-for minions in the legal and law enforcement bureaucracies did his bidding without question out of an appreciation for the money and favors he would bestow upon them— but most importantly because of his well-earned reputation for crushing his perceived enemies with a lethal combination of institutional power and a level of cruelty that was undiluted by anything that could be remotely considered humane. He intimidated everyone that stood between him and what he wanted with power that was absolute and a heart without mercy.

All of this, one might justifiably assume, would be more than sufficient to qualify him for the title of chief villain in this story. However, I am obligated to add to these impressive qualifications the fact that this particular elected official was a lifelong, unrepentant, violent spousal abuser.

Violence

I was in a biker bar after work sometime in the eighties. I had just ordered a second beer when a big drunk non-biker dude started yelling to no one in particular. He was pissed off about an incident that happened earlier that day or possibly twenty years ago. The specifics were buried beneath the secret slurring dialect of the inebriated and lost to the world. The one thing that we patrons were able to determine was that he was begging to have his ass kicked in a bar full of people for whom the kicking of ass was a fairly routine enterprise.

I have a long and complicated relationship with violence. The first time I was slapped in the face by a stranger for no reason I was five years old and pushing a tricycle. By the time I graduated high school I had seen so many big people beat the crap out of so many not big people that the memories have all melded together into one bloody blur. I'm sure that the prospect of being on the receiving end of daily violence without the physical attributes necessary for the occasional victory is why I became funny. "You're funny. I'll kill you last." It also taught me how to be intensely focused in situations like this.

Back to the bar.

I knew from previous experience in these matters that I had perhaps two minutes to predict if the patrons were going to ignore him or if the furniture was likely to become airborne. I recalled that earlier in the evening the guy on the drunk dude's left was complaining about his wife. I called the bartender over, slid my beer across the bar and asked him to put it on ice for me. I told him that I'd be back. I left, walked to another bar, had a drink and returned fifty minutes later to reclaim my beer and hear about the fight.

With the first loud sound from the angry drunk I had gone

into survival mode. The primary function of this headspace is to assess the probability of escalation. No escalation no threat. The overexposure to anger and violence in my formative years combined with the observational skills I was forced to learn during the three-year hitchhiking adventure I took after graduating high school formed me into a person who constantly gathers and cross-references information on everyone who is close enough to me to pose a threat.

A drunk guy yelling is just noise. A drunk guy yelling next to a guy whose home life is shitty enough for him to bark about it to strangers is the perfect combination for a fight. I guessed that the married guy would not be able to resist the temptation to release some of his pent-up frustration upon the skull of the noisemaker. My options were to leave or stay and risk becoming collateral damage.

Survival mode shuts down every part of my brain that isn't actively contributing to the goal of emerging from the incident unscathed. When I returned to reclaim my beer-on-ice, the fight was over. I then allowed the storyteller in me to emerge from the locked room where he had been ordered to remain until the hostilities ceased. I spent the rest of that day thinking about the back stories of these two combatants. What were their childhoods like? What happened to them during the earlier part of their lives that brought them to this moment in this place at this time?

If Jordan Walsh is threatening your family and the financial well-being of your small business by refusing to pay you for your work, thinking about his life story and speculating on the early events that that shaped him into the adult he became is counterproductive. Empathy and curiosity are distractions. They won't help you get paid. But the job was over for us. Our payment was certain. In a matter of minutes this experience would be relegated to history.

Back Story

Moments climb into the wet cement of a child's forming personality and remain until the years solidify them there.

A trembling embrace with your twin brother in a dark closet as your bodies jolt at the loud thumping sound followed by a short yelp—your five-year-old hearts beating rapidly against each other's.

That moment when you think you hear the front door slam and you inch out into the bedroom light trusting each other as one of you slowly turns the doorknob and you poke your heads into the chilling silence of the hallway.

Walking down the stairs to the living room with the beautiful bravery of children unable to defend themselves, relieved to see that your mother is alive but boiling with rage too big to be contained inside your small body as you see her holding an ice pack to her swollen jaw.

The look in her eye complex beyond comprehension containing and revealing so many things: love, fear, shame and all that is held within a heart burdened with the inability to spare you this moment—especially the knowledge of how irreversibly it is defining your future.

These are the moments that dominate your formative years. They are the reasons why you only play superhero games—superheroes who rely on each other to save the world and the girl from Evil. And Evil never wins. He is always crushed. And you have your brother, who knows the feel of your terrified heart pressed against his own, to savor these victories with.

*****

Both Jordan and his twin brother Jonathan started their own businesses right out of college. To the surprise of no one who knew them, they were both millionaires before their thirtieth birthday.

Early on Jonathan's business needed an infusion of capital and in what turned out to be a fatal mistake he accepted an investment from his father. To the surprise of no one who knew them, the father and son fought incessantly about the way the business should be run. The dad, again quite predictably, used his connections and his knowledge of and unfettered access to the inner workings of government and law to bring to bear tremendous pressure upon Jonathan in a series of lawsuits and unspoken, but unambiguous, intimidations.

Jonathan, being cut from the same cloth, countersued. In the course of their legal wrangling he made it clear that he was willing, and uniquely able, to expose the decades-long abuses of power by the elder statesman/patriarch. When the opposing legal firm countered that such information would be inadmissible, Jonathan sent word directly to their client that he was willing to leak the detailed history of corruption to the media.

One month later Jonathan was murdered. His father was interviewed one time by police detectives. The case is currently unsolved.

Sitting alone in the dashboard light of the van the storyteller/speculator/maker-upper of back stories in me is shattered. So much so that the survivor in me intervenes and dispatches him back to quarantine for fear that further speculation on what the murder of Jonathan did to the heart of Jordan might cause him permanent psychological damage.

The driver's door opened and broke the spell. Dennis looked like he had seen a ghost. He was pale and wore an air of bewilderment. He did not speak. He threw the van into reverse, turned it around and drove away.

"You okay?" I asked. There was an uncomfortably long pause

and he replied, "No." My first thought was the obvious one—that now that the job was over there would be a big fight over getting paid but I knew that payment was secured by the GC and if that were the problem Dennis would be angry. He was not angry.

This Can Not Be Happening

We drove half the distance home in an uncomfortable silence before Dennis said, "I have no idea what just happened." After a long pause he continued, "He was there. I didn't know. How could I …" I interjected, "I love you like a brother but I have to tell you that going back there to hide a body is going to seriously test this friendship." When he failed to laugh or even smile a chill shot through me unlike any I have ever known. Then, he continued as if he hadn't heard me. "I had forgotten to rewire the panel. He was all over me—just like the last time. He was right in my face. I couldn't get away from him."

"Don't tell me this! This can not be happening!" The fact that I was yelling seemed to bring him back into the front seat of the van with me. He pulled over, looked me square in the eyes and continued, "It happened so fast. I felt like a cornered rat. I didn't know what to do. I blurted out, 'I've worked my ass off for you on this job.' That only made him madder. Then, and I have no idea why, I said, 'I left a Christmas party with my family two days ago to come here for a wiring inspection that everyone, including you, knew was not going to happen. My family doesn't live around here. I only get to see them once a year and I pulled myself away from them for three hours for nothing … and family is really important to me.'

"And as soon as I said that all the blood seemed to drain out of his face. He took two steps back. He looked like a little boy who had just been punched in the stomach. He backed up another step and said, 'I apologize. You're right, family is important. Go home. We'll deal with this after Christmas.' I backed out of the room and as we were staring at each other across the threshold he said, and honestly I'm not sure if I dreamed this, he said, 'No, really. I mean it. Family is important. Thanks for your work. Have a good holiday.'"

AN OLD MAN'S DREAM

What am I doing back here and who are you? Are you me at seventeen? How cliché.

No, you big dope. Blue eyes? Blonde hair? This is going to be a colossal waste of time if you can't pay attention to what's happening. You are right though, a dream sequence taking place in your childhood kitchen with your seventeen-year-old self would be the kind of movie we would both click away from as soon as we became aware of the pedestrian premise.

I'm your grandson's grandson. The eyes and hair are because your progeny kept mating with non-Mediterraneans until all the brown eyes and curly dark Greek hair was completely washed out of your bloodline. Sorry.

Great. So, what do you want Blondie? Are you here to tell me how horrible the future is? Whoever thought up the story line in this dream has got to get off the weed. This reeks of one of those stoner ideas that sounds brilliant at four in the morning but has to slink back into dumb idea land when illuminated by the sober light of day.

Now I know where my family's attitude problem comes from. Look old man, I'm the age you were when you left this kitchen to become whatever it is you became. You saw the world a certain way when you left. You learned a bunch of stuff in the following decades that changed your view on some if not all of those things. I'm here to ask you to tell me, from the great lofty perch of cantankerous old-mandom, what priceless pearls of wisdom you wish some ornery old goat had imparted to you when you were my age.

Well, there's no denying this is a dream now is there? Even though I am lying in my bed with my eyes rolling back and forth at the deepest level of REM sleep, I still know that teenagers don't ask old men for advice. It just doesn't happen. But hey, what the hell, I'll play along. You want some old man wisdom? Let's start with the ocean.

Seriously? You are going to use this once-in-a-lifetime moment that is unleashed from the tyranny of time, where the year 2021 can interact with 1974 and provide you the opportunity to converse with a descendant that is a minimum of fifty years from being born, to talk about the ocean? It wouldn't occur to you to maybe drop a little knowledge on love or the meaning of life? Damn! I gotta say, I'm a little disappointed here Donny Boy.

Shut up. I hate to be the one to break the news to you but disappointing a fictional dream character means fuck all to me.

The ocean exists to remind the self-absorbed that the universe doesn't think you're special. It doesn't give a shit about you or your problems. It doesn't rejoice in your meager accomplishments. The ocean voices the opinion of the universe that you are, in the vernacular of my father, "a pimple on the ass of progress." Next time you feel that the world is lined up against you and that your existence is any more important than the zillions of other fleshy, self-aware bipeds that lived and died on this tiny planet in this miniscule galaxy, go to the ocean and listen to the waves crashing against the seawall. There is a proclamation in the form of a rhetorical question in the sound of the waves. Listen carefully and you will hear these words: "Who's bad?" The ocean is bad and it has a message for you. "You don't matter."

We don't matter … except to each other. Joseph Campbell, having, one would suspect, grown weary of being asked about the meaning of life, said, "Life has no meaning. Each of us has meaning and we bring it to life. It is a waste to be asking the question when you are the answer."

That's some deep shit right there, ain't it?

Make your evolution as a human being your primary focus while you're here. The more evolved you become, the more you can contribute to the lives of the people you are spinning through space with. We can, if we choose to, be as important and impactful in the lives of those we love as we are inconsequential to the ocean. If it turns out that doesn't actually matter, at least it will look and feel good from the end.

How's that?

Weird … but surprisingly engaging. Go on.

Okay, I think I can actually get into this. Here's one I really wish someone had told me back then. I can't presume that you are as observant as your forefathers—you know, with all the watering down of our good DNA through decades of impulsive breeding. But, in case some of my thoughtful genetic markers did survive the gentrification of my future bloodline and you are observant, I've got a good one for you.

I could always tell what people wanted me to be and what they hoped their inaccurate version of me would say and do in a given situation. Whenever it suited my needs, I would do my best to become and behave like their naive expectations—not forever and not for their benefit—but so I could manipulate them into giving me what I wanted. This is an awesome power to put into the hands of a horny teenager with drug and alcohol issues. Whenever I was in trouble, I used it to get teachers, principals and other adults to view me in accordance with their vision of my potential to become a productive member of society, in the hope that they would bestow leniency upon me. I also applied this skill to get people to share the last of their drugs and alcohol with me and, as you might imagine, to make the voluntary unbuttoning of one's own blouse on my behalf seem like the right thing to do.

Where'd you go old man?

Sorry. I was just allowing the lizard part of my brain to indulge a few youthful memories … before I tell you how wrong this all is.

Later … much, much later, when I was older and a bit more thoughtful, I began to feel uncomfortable with the way manipulative selfishness made me feel. Slowly…very, very slowly, I started experimenting with using my observational skills to actually help people as opposed to making them believe I was helping them while I got them to give me what I wanted. It turned out that the same tool set that enabled me to decipher and mimic a person's optimistic vision of me could be used to see the underlying issues that might be the cause of that person's suffering. Helping people and not wanting something in return made me feel good. And feeling good without the use of artificial stimulants slowly (very, very slowly) became my drug of choice.

If someone had told me this at your age, I would still have used my observational abilities to fulfill my immediate wants and needs but maybe, empowered with this knowledge, I might have stopped being a dick a little sooner. Who knows?

Wait. Are you texting?

Yes Gramps. I'm calling a hovercraft taxi to rescue me from this conversation. I'm kidding. I'm actually texting a girl I met last week. I just asked her to meet me when this dream is over. I'm hoping she'll be wearing that white blouse that buttons up the front.

That's funny. It's going to make it harder for me to keep

disliking you, but I'm pretty resourceful. I think I can muster the intestinal fortitude to rise to the occasion.

Up to now I have been justifiably cynical about this encounter. The mediocre (some might say lazy) premise was just a bit too much for me to take seriously. I am/was/whatever ... a writer you know. But, as is often the case with me, I am now beginning to embrace the idea I initially, reflexively, recoiled from.

I know nothing about my grandfather's father. I would love to meet him and learn firsthand about his life and times. What challenges did he overcome? What got the best of him? What crap did he have to deal with that was endemic to his time and not an issue for future generations? When he was on his way out what was he proud of—what were his regrets? We feel these people in our blood but we know nothing about them except what is in the historical record—birth and death date and names of spouses and descendants. We can't know what they loved or hated, how they suffered or struggled, how their personal challenges shaped their view of the world, or what wisdom they acquired during their short journey from womb to grave.

Damn. I'm getting weepy now. This is my M.O.—lead with sarcasm, end with sentimentality. The harder the shell, the softer the caramel filling. I'm losing it. Give me a minute.

Okay. I'm feeling a strong urge to talk about writing. There are entire sections of the library (they still have libraries, right?) that are devoted to the mental health benefits of writing. (A lot of good they do for a world full of brains that for generations have been rewired to shut down after reading one hundred and forty characters.) Anyway, here's my bite-size, dumbed down exposé.

Writing is cheaper than therapy. You pay a therapist to get you to describe your trauma. Then he or she asks you how you feel about your trauma. Then he or she encourages you to think about how you can change the way you view and feel about the trauma. Total price to you or your insurance company is enough for a down payment on a house.

Write about that shit. Ask yourself how that shit you wrote about makes you feel. Think about how you can change how you feel about that shit. Change how you feel about it. Eliminate the middleman.

Save tens of thousands of dollars. Buy a house with the money. Live happily ever after.

Gramps, has anyone ever called you a character? You are very entertaining. I'm enjoying the hell out of you. So much so that I'm not going to list the dozens of important caveats that your colossal oversimplification of the relationship between therapist and patient has conveniently glossed over. Because introducing academic nuance to that colorful display of working-class bluster would be like straightening out the facial features on a surrealist portrait.

Hmmm. Did you just dis me? Did I just get dissed by a wet-behind-the-ears, yet-to-be-born dream apparition? This is the best damn dream I've ever had. Where was I? I remember now.

When you write, you connect with the part of you that was there before the world planted a crappy, heavy metal garage band between you and your heart. Writing is how you unplug the amplifiers, shut down the shrieking of the skinny, greasy, angry lead singer so you can listen to your heart and remember who you are.

Damn! No! No! I'm waking up! I'm not done yet. I'll never find my way back here again. Wait. Wait. I know how to not wake up. I've done it lots of times. Waking up is a process. If I stop the process before it goes too far I can get back. Just pull the pillow over my head and focus on resisting consciousness. The 1970s were an excellent training ground for resisting consciousness. No wonder I'm so good at this. Back down the tunnel—all the way back.

Okay. I'm back. Reality averted.

There is no telling how long I can stay here this time so before I continue to elaborate on the benefits of writing, I want to say that I hope you have as interesting and fulfilling a life as I have had. I don't know why human beings are so emotionally connected to their ancestors and descendants. It probably has to do with the way we evolved in tribes. Google it.

Anyway, I'm having a ton of "feels" right now in the super-gooey caramel filling area beneath my crusty shell and I don't want to be yanked out of here without telling you that I love you.

Thanks. I appreciate it. But I think you should say what you want to say to me before I have to go back to having not been born and you have to go back to being an old man with lots to say that no one wants to hear.

Right. I knew my descendants would be smart. Okay, where was I?

Write. Do it in cursive. I can't believe they stopped teaching cursive in school. In cursive you hardly have to lift your pen off the paper. Cursive is designed to accommodate the flow of ideas. Teach yourself to let what you want to say pour out onto the page. Don't edit. Let it flow. Edit later. The reason I consider it a felony to not teach children how to write in cursive has nothing to do with them not being able to read the original Bill of Rights. That's just a piece of parchment with noble ideas written on it that politicians claim ownership of just before they use it to wipe their ass.

The reason you should write in cursive is that the part of you that knows what you were born to do—that knows who you were before the world turned up the amps on modern life's dreadful music—lives in your heart. It pumps ideas to your brain. Your brain sends the idea through your blood, down your arm to your fingers where that idea travels from your heart to the ink in your pen and then out onto a page and into the world. Cursive is the natural fluid extension of an idea that travels through blood. You write it. You read it. You remember who you are and who you were born to be.

Write. It will center you through the cacophony of modern life for free.

I can tell I'm going to wake up soon. I think it's because I have to pee. I feel bad that you inherited my snark and my attitude problem. Sorry about that. Let me try to make it up to you by squeezing a few distilled gobs of worldly wisdom into this dream/play that might prove useful to you as you navigate the shitstorm that the combination of a world run by the impressively unevolved and your regrettable genetic predisposition for unreasonableness has in store for you.

One. Write, write, write. Have I said that enough? Two. Include kindness in your decision making whenever possible but don't be afraid to punch someone in the nose when kindness is not an option. There are other bloodlines that are more evolved and will turn the other cheek. Your family's blood hasn't gotten there yet. Three. Don't do business with deeply religious people. They can't be trusted to do the right thing if doing the right thing requires questioning doctrine. They will screw you over and justify their behavior by pointing to a paragraph of a book that was written when physicians practiced bloodletting and fathers chose husbands for their daughters when they turned twelve. Four. When you meet a kind person who is strong under pressure, and makes you laugh, marry that person. Five. Be gentle with yourself. Learn from your mistakes, don't use them as an excuse to devalue your worth—but don't keep making them. Six. Laugh.

Laugh?

Yes. Every day without exception. It will do more for your

long-term mental health than yoga, therapy, meditation, a noble cause, and slowly unbuttoned blouses combined.

That should have been the end, right? The credits should be rolling now. And the audience should be on their way to the box office to demand a refund. Why am I not waking up?

I have no idea old man. If I were in a movie theater I could, I suppose, just nod off and spare myself the inevitable oncoming assault to my intelligence that I now fear shall ensue. But the fact that I have thus far been the recipient of this master class in condescension during sleep has removed from me my most reliable escape hatch.

Again, very clever, but—as I have learned is often the case with witty contributions from my new favorite apparition—not especially helpful.

It's one thing to feel the kind of trepidation, described in a previous section, from fear that a dream might be ending too soon. It's quite another to be panicked over the possibility that it might never end.

I never thought of that.

No one has. So, since for the life of me I can't think of a single thing more that my decades have taught me that might be useful to a teenager, and since we're sitting here like we're both waiting for our best friends to pull up and rescue us from a bad first date, how about I use whatever remaining time the invisible dream gods have over allocated to this unfortunate enterprise to bore you into a serious contemplation of suicide with a bunch of thoughts I've had recently about being old?

I'll take your silence as your consent and ignore that "God save me" look on your face.

What do you think an old man wants? Stop. Don't answer that. It would take weeks for you to give voice to and for me to endure all the wiseass crap you would spout—smaller prostate, brain that doesn't repeat the same story over and over, functional phallus, brain that doesn't repeat the same story over and over—I get it. We've already established your irreverence and predictable sense of humor. Let me rephrase the question.

How can an old man who has lived an interesting life find a way to feel useful in his waning years? Everyone desperately wants to feel useful. It's one of those annoying "being human" things. Seriously, you *are* aware that I actually dreamed you into existence for the sole purpose of creating a situation where in a fabricated scenario I might enjoy the pleasure of pontificating to a person who is at least pretending to be interested?

Try to keep up.

In the unlikely event that you aren't killed by one of the life-threatening scenarios that your abysmal decision making will produce, and you live long enough for that tragic blonde mane to turn gray, here's something I have learned that might be worthy of your future consideration.

Most of the knowledge and wisdom that people acquire during a lifetime ends up buried with their bodies. If the man with life's least impressive resume—who used his waking hours between birth and death to fight, fuck, work, and get drunk with not a single moment of introspection—if that guy (variations of whom I have been blessed to work beside on many construction sites) could reveal in detail just one thing that he learned before embarking on a long career in the unfortunate business of becoming compost, the benefit for subsequent generations would be immeasurable.

If all of the people buried in just one mid-size graveyard could teach us the trade they practiced or the story of how they found the strength to overcome their life's greatest challenge, or the thing the world taught them that no one ever bothered to ask them about, the human race would be so appreciably advanced as to be unrecognizable to its present-day constituency.

I'll pay a hundred dollars and a half ounce of killer bud to anyone that can call my phone and wake me up right now.

Good one. I have to say that I'm starting to enjoy this. Shall I continue? Let's begin with the premise that feeling as good as possible as often as possible is a good thing. We're human. We survived in groups. In an attempt to ensure the survival of the species our evolutionary biology has learned to reward us by releasing feelgood chemicals to our brains when we belong and contribute to the tribe. It reserves the greatest and highest quality (or purest, if you, as just indicated, prefer contemporary drug parlance) explosions of joy juice for the waning years of an interesting life when you get to take what you have learned and gift it to the tribe on your way out the door. What's the point of learning all this stuff and overcoming all of modern life's bullshit if every subsequent generation has to go blindly through the same struggles because you couldn't figure out how not to be the type of insufferable old man that no one could tolerate listening to?

The first job in pursuit of the big mentoring dopamine buzz is to figure out how to behave in a way that might induce in people the suspicion that you might have something of value to say.

Underneath the rolling eyes of young people is a need to be heard … and, as surprising as it seems, a need to be appreciated by elders. The problem is they likely have never been in the company of a grownup who was worthy of their time.

You can't fake worthiness to young people. It is true that their decision making can be so colossally bad at times that one might justifiably assume that they have not yet recovered from a serious head injury. But the interesting thing about humans that are not fully formed is that they can be brilliantly insightful and adept at navigating one challenge and gobsmackingly ineffective in another. Within the realm of detecting feigned worthiness in adults, I am of the opinion that many young people, who might appear clueless to the cursory glance of elders predisposed to that assumption, are often savants.

As is evidenced by the look on my face at this very moment.

Shut up.

So you can't fake it. You have to change yourself into something unlike what they have learned to disdain. Start by trashing the idea that years lived equate wisdom. They don't. Even the most cursory look at the old bastards running the world will reveal all the evidence you'll need to disabuse you of this untenable notion. It is possible, and quite common, to live long and learn almost nothing of real value.

Every thing you learned got placed into a "Forever True" file in your brain. Open that folder and separate the contents into two categories. The first is for knowledge based on Shakespearean themes—love, greed, power, lust, deceit. Whatever you learned along the way about being human is probably still true. Because, despite their inability to remove their eyes from a hologram world that lives inside their phones, today's humans are, at least for now, still human and will respond to the aforementioned subjects in exactly the same way they did in my man Shakespeare's time.

Everything else needs a separate folder titled "To Be Reviewed with Fresh Eyes." Teach yourself to question everything you thought was true that isn't tied to the nature of being human. The world that existed when I learned something in the seventies is gone.

And for this my generation gives thanks.

Many of those "truths" had an expiration date stamped on their head that I never noticed till I dusted them off and moved them into the sunlight of this current decade. If, in modern light and with fresh eyes, they are still relevant and useful to someone who never wore bellbottoms, I keep 'em. If not, I dump 'em. Then I ask a young person what is true now regarding the subject of my newly discarded obsolete truths.

When an observant young person sees you reevaluating the annoying old crap that they hear from all your tiresome peers, it might just kindle a spark in their biological need to be mentored by an elder. When you ask them what they think about something important or, even better, ask them to help you understand something that is of their world, you will, in all likelihood, be the first adult who has ever done so and the dynamics of the relationship will be forever changed.

If you combine these pearls of knowledge I have so articulately and foolishly cast before swine (no offense) with the willingness to say "I don't know. Let me think about that for a while," you will separate yourself from all the other preachy, condescending human antiquities that young people are obliged to endure. With a little luck thereafter you may become one of the privileged few who find a willing ear for their hard-earned truths while in pursuit of life's most intoxicating serotonin pleasure center blast. It's all about the buzz Blondie.

This already feels super preachy so I'm going to move on without expounding on how hurtful it is to tell young people that the world was better before they were born and that they missed all the good stuff. But believe me I could do another hour on what an unforgivable abuse of power that sort of talk is and how much I hate it when I see my generation engage in this felonious falsity with young people. The time you're living in is the greatest time there has ever been no matter when it is. There is only one minute—and if you're not living in it—you're nowhere at all.

I've gotta go. My bladder is demanding that I be awake for our nightly trip to the bathroom.

I'm gonna miss you. Bye.

Acknowledgments

The brain I brought with me fifteen years ago to combat the formidable intimidation of the blank page during the writing of my first book was young and battle-ready.

Although in the interim the blank page became a more fearsome opponent, the brain I brought into the fray this time was a shell of his former self. I wooed him out of retirement for this one last battle, but he no longer fit into his uniform and looked like a warrior whose glory was behind him.

Everything took longer with this dude. He needed twice the amount of coffee and sleep and hydration than in the past but when sufficiently rested, hydrated, and caffeinated, he not only rose to the occasion but made up for his dramatic decrease in stamina with some worldliness that was not available to his younger self all those years ago.

So I'd like to begin these acknowledgements by thanking my parents for the genetic gift of a vascular system that keeps blood flowing to the brains of their descendants in their plaque-filled golden years.

Writing is a solitary endeavor. Making the words that are born in solitude live up to their potential and flow in a way that creates a good experience for the reader requires more than just an editor. Terence Hegarty is a world-class editor and so much more. His patience and guidance and gentle persistence are so integral to my writing process that I shudder at the thought of not having him as a partner for every sentence I write. You, dear reader, are the beneficiary of his frequent notes to me saying, "This is okay, but you can do better." Thank you Terence.

Thanks to Ann Marie Catabia for creating the wonderful artwork with her brilliant artist's eye.

Thanks to Jim Infantino for his patience and his attention to detail in the formatting of this book.

Thanks to Mark Steele for his back cover photo and for all the video projects we have created over these many years.

And thanks to Skip Bowes who clicked a photo of Theresa and I when he dropped us off after a visit in Amarillo, Texas in 1975. It is the only photograph of us from our three years of hitchhiking and we treasure it.

And …

Speaking of Theresa … I don't know how I wound up falling more and more in love with this woman with every passing year. I always knew I wanted to grow old with her. I hoped it would happen. It did. And I intend to enjoy and appreciate every minute we have together.

Two Vagabonds in Disguise

Lyrics

Didn't I know you in seventy-four
You were eighteen and out of control
Hitchhiking far and wide
For ten months at a time
Sleeping by the side of the road
All day long you would walk
Hiking boots, Birkenstocks
You lived on black beans and rice
The wind in your hair my friend
The freedom you knew back then
Still can be seen in the eyes
Of a waitress with two kids by her side

Didn't I know you in seventy-four
You were wild you were out of your mind
Ram Dass and Alan Watts
All night in truck stops
Your poetry on highway signs

The road was your teacher then
Sleeping on beaches and
Reaching for things in the sky
The wind in your hair my friend
The freedom you knew back then
Still can be seen in the eyes of
A night watchman with two kids at his side

When it's midnight – I work the graveyard shift
Daylight – I sleep you watch the kids
Noontime – You're ironing your uniform
Midnight – You return, leave the engine on
A kiss and a hug at the door
A long time since seventy-four

I left a note for you
A few things we need to do
It's hanging up on the wall
It says, power bill must be paid
Both the kids have been bathed
Your brother from Florida called
Around and around it goes
Where it goes, no one knows
Put your feet up for a while
There's wine in the fridge, I'm late
Give me a kiss
You know in that slow-moving smile
I still see that vagabond child

When its midnight – I work the graveyard shift
Daylight – I sleep you watch the kids
Noontime – You're ironing your uniform
Midnight – You return, leave the engine on
A kiss, a hug, and a sigh
Two vagabonds in disguise

Guitar Chords:
C G C F
F C G F G C

Copyright Don White 1982
Lumperboy Music

Addendum

A Baby Monster and
the Boy Who Did Not Like Pickles

In 2015 I started performing at storytelling festivals. Because these events are family friendly, all tellers are obliged to perform for children. I'd never done it. I'd never even thought about it. I remember thinking that I'd be less intimidated by a bar full of drunk bikers than a classroom full of fourth graders.

But I had to learn. I spent six months taking classes and learning everything I could about kids and how to hold their attention.

I now have a deep appreciation for children's performers and the challenges they are subjected to that no other entertainers ever have to deal with.

During my immersion into this world, I challenged myself to write a children's story. I was intrigued by the idea of writing a story where the parents had problems. I hoped I could write something that would be funny and honest and kind to all the characters.

This is what I came up with.

Once upon a time there was a boy named Oscar who liked to eat pizza. He also liked peanut butter, cucumbers, tomatoes and apples but he DID NOT like pickles. He didn't not like pickles a little. He did not like pickles at all.

Every day Oscar's mother walked with him through the scary monster forest to school. (This story takes place in the olden days and back then all children had to walk through scary forests.)

Some of the people in the town told Oscar and his mother that monsters were mean and bad but Oscar and his mom saw lots of them on their daily walks and even though these monsters were forty feet tall, very loud and very hairy they were always friendly to Oscar and his mom because monsters loved their children and they could see how much Oscar's mom loved Oscar.

One day in the deepest, darkest, spookiest part of the monster forest they heard a sound they had never heard before. It sounded a little like a monster growl but instead of the big loud GROWL they were used to hearing it was a high-pitched squeaky little growl.

They followed the sound to the base of a monster tree (those are the trees that the monsters live in and since monsters grow to be forty feet tall you can imagine that the trees they live in are very big—maybe a thousand feet tall or a hexaca, texaca jillion feet tall). There at the base of a hexaca-texaca-jillion foot tall tree they saw a little fuzzy baby monster that was about as big as an apple (not a monster apple because those are as big as basketballs) but a regular boy size apple.

When Oscar looked into the purple eyes of the baby monster he knew two things: That the baby was lost—that he needed something to eat and that he would name him Fuzzball. I know, that's three things. I did that on purpose because I wanted to see if you were paying attention but you're very smart and I don't think I can trick you.

Oscar and his mom yelled as loud as they could up toward the trees, "Did any monsters lose a baby?" No one answered so they did it again—maybe if we all do it together it will be loud enough so the parents could hear it even if they are so high in the trees that their heads are in the clouds. Let's try it. "Did any monsters lose a baby?" No one answered.

Oscar's Mother said, "We can't leave this baby here. We'll bring him home, keep him warm by the fireplace and feed him. Then every day when we walk through the woods we'll try to find his parents." Oscar said, "Fuzzball, how does that sound to you?" To which Fuzzball replied, "growl, growl" (because he was a baby monster and that was the only word he knew how to say). So Oscar's mom picked up Fuzzball who was as big as an apple—(not a monster apple because those are as big as a ... basketball? No, a beach ball and a basketball). And she put him gently in her purse and she and Oscar continued walking toward home.

They were almost to the edge of the scary monster forest when they came to a tree that had a group of monsters in it and they were singing this song:

Monster Tea, Monster Tea
We love to drink our monster tea
It makes us want to dance and sing
We love to drink our monster tea

Oscar and his mom yelled, "Did any monsters lose a baby?" The singing stopped and a monster growled (which sounded scary but that's just the way they talk) "No. None of us has lost a baby." Oscar's mom said, "Well we found one and we're going

262 The Hitchhiking Years and Four Other Stories

to feed it and keep it warm and we'll come back every day to try to find his parents. "OK," they growled and went back to singing their monster tea song.

When they got home Oscar gave Fuzzball a slice of his favorite pizza. Fuzzball took one bite and spit it out on the floor making this sound, "Pitui." Then Oscar gave him a peanut butter sandwich. "Pitui, pitui." Two pituis? "Fuzzball doesn't like peanut butter more than he doesn't like pizza," said Oscar. "Maybe he just doesn't like foods that begin with the letter P." So he gave him a cucumber, a tomato, and an apple. "Pitui, pitui, pitui."

Fuzzball was getting very angry and sad which made Oscar feel terrible because he loved the little guy but he couldn't understand why he wouldn't eat any of the yummiest foods in the world (according to Oscar).

Oscar's mom said, "We must learn what foods are best to feed to a baby monster." So she decided to look it up on the internet but because this was the olden days when there were no computers or cell phones and the internet was made out of paper. She turned the pages of the giant internet book. And there on page one thousand six hundred and fifty-two of the chapter on monster's diet she read that the only food that baby monsters ever eat is ... can you guess? Yes. PICKLES!

This information made Oscar so angry that he fell on the floor, started spinning in a circle and screaming, "I don't like pickles. I don't want to see them. I don't want to touch them. I do not want them on my plate near my pizza and apples and I DO NOT want to feed them to Fuzzball!"

When Oscar's mother picked him up off the floor his arms were still waving and he was still screaming "No pickles, no pickles, no pickles!" She plunked him down at the table and said,

"Oscar, it is okay for you to not like pickles but it is not even a little bit ok for you to scream and spin in circles on the floor for any reason. This situation with Fuzzball is a little bit complicated and screaming and spinning only makes a complicated situation more complicated. Look at Fuzzball's face," she said. Oscar looked and could tell that all the yelling made him sad and scared.

Oscar's mom said, "You need to decide whether you love Fuzzball more than you do not love pickles." She placed a big jar of pickles on the table, opened the cover and walked away.

Oscar stared at the jar. Then he looked at Fuzzball whose purple eyes were wide with excitement. He was smiling and bouncing up and down in his chair like a rubber ball. (Not a monster size rubber because those are as big as … beach balls? No. Those big rubber balls with the handle on them that you sit on and bounce across the room … and beach balls and basketballs.)

Oscar went to the cabinet and grabbed the fork with the longest handle. Then he held his nose with one hand and stretched his arm out as far from his body as possible and plunged that fork into the jar and into a big yucky pickle. Then keeping that pickle as far away from his nose as possible he dropped the fork with the pickle still stuck to it on a plate that his mother had put in front of Fuzzball.

When Fuzzball ate the pickle he grew two inches, smiled a happy monster baby smile and fell asleep.

Oscar and his mother brought Fuzzball with them every day on their walk through the forest and every day they would yell, "Did any monsters lose a baby?" Well, Oscar and his mom would yell that but Fuzzball just yelled, "Growl, growl, growl. Growl, growl, growl, growl, growl, growl." Because he was a baby and that was the only word he could say. But no one ever answered their calls.

In the year that followed you might think that Oscar learned to love pickles. He didn't. But he did eventually learn to feed them to Fuzzball without holding his nose and being angry about it.

When Fuzzball got bigger and learned how to talk he and Oscar would eat lunch together every day. And every day Oscar would have pizza or peanut butter, cucumbers, tomatoes or apples and Fuzzball would have broccoli? No, pickles.

Each day Oscar would say, "Fuzzball, you are my best friend and I love you but I will never understand why you like the taste of yucky, gucky, stinky pickles." And Fuzzball would say, "Oscar, you are my best friend and I love you but I will never understand why you do not like the taste of yummy delicious pickles and why you DO like the taste of stinky, smelly, yucky pizza and peanut butter." And then they would laugh and laugh.

Because Fuzzball grew two inches every time he ate a pickle (and he ate three pickles every day) he got so big that he could hardly fit through the door to Oscar's house. Oscar and his mom were planning to find him a tree in the monster forest and help him build his own house. But because they weren't monsters, were not forty feet tall and had never built a monster home before they were pretty sure that they would need an adult monster to help them build it.

It was at this time that two adult monsters walked into Oscar's yard and knocked on his door. They didn't knock with their hands of course because they were forty feet tall and would have to lie on the ground to do that. Instead they knocked on Oscar's door with their toes.

When Oscar and his mother opened the door they were staring at the kneecaps of two giant hairy monsters.

Oscar got a ladder, leaned it against the house, climbed to

the roof and then to the top of the chimney so he was face to face with the two giant monsters and said, "My name is Oscar." Just then Fuzzball squeezed out of the front door. Oscar noticed that when the adult monsters saw Fuzzball they looked uncomfortable and nervous.

They looked at Fuzzball and then they looked at Oscar and said, "We are Fuzzball's mother and father. One year ago when you found him we were having a lot of problems because every day we would drink monster tea. It made us dance and sing all night but it also made it so we didn't have time to shop for pickles. We knew that it would take a long time for us to fix all our problems so we decided to put Fuzzball where you and your mom would find him because we saw how nice and kind and friendly you were and we saw that your mom took really good care of you. And we wanted our baby to have a great life. It was a very hard decision."

Oscar thought that these monsters were here to take Fuzzball away from him and his mom and he GOT ANGRY. He was so angry that he was about to fall on the floor, spin in circles and scream at them but he realized he was on top of the chimney, on top of the roof and there was no floor to fall and spin on. He wanted to yell at them and say, "You can not come here and take Fuzzball away from me. He is my best friend. I fed him stinky, yucky, gucky pickles every day for a year!" But before he could say any of that he looked into the faces of the monsters and he could see that they were sad and disappointed with themselves. Then he looked at his mom and he could see that she looked sad and nervous AND then he looked at Fuzzball and Fuzzball's face seemed to show all the feelings that everyone was having. He looked sad, happy, angry, scared, but mostly confused.

Oscar realized that this was a complicated situation and that everyone had a lot of different feelings about it and he remembered that his mother once said, "Screaming and spinning only make a complicated situation more complicated." So he decided not to yell because it might make everyone cry including Fuzzball, so instead he asked, "Are you here to take my best friend away from me?"

The two monsters looked at each other and smiled. Then they said, "No, Oscar, we came here to thank you and your mom for taking such good care of him while we were trying to stop drinking monster tea and trying to fix our other problems. It was a very hard decision for us to give him up to you but seeing how big and strong and hairy and full of pickles he is we know that we made the right decision. And we wanted to let you know that we do not drink monster tea anymore and that all of you are welcome to visit us in the monster forest" (they don't call it the scary monster forest because of course, monsters don't think that monsters are scary).

Fuzzball looked at Oscar and his mom and then he gave the adult monsters a big hug. He said, "Oscar and his mom are my family now but I think we can all be great friends. In fact, I am almost too big to fit in the house anymore and I need to build my own house in a monster tree. But I've never done it before and Oscar and his mom are not even big enough to reach the lowest branches" ("because they don't eat enough pickles," he whispered). "So maybe you could help me?"

They said, "Yes, of course we would love, love, love to help you build a house. In fact there is a monster tree right next to ours that would be perfect."

Oscar looked at all the faces, his mom's, Fuzzball's, and the monsters', and he could see that they were all smiling and happy. And even though he couldn't see his own face he was sure that it had a big smile on it.

Everyone in Oscar's two families worked together and built Fuzzball a nice house. They even added a ladder that reached from the lowest branch (that was as high as the roof of a house) to the ground so Oscar and his mom could climb up whenever they wanted to visit and they wanted to visit a lot. Often they would come over to Fuzzball's new house for lunch. Oscar's mom would bring pizza and peanut butter sandwiches for Oscar and for Fuzzball she would bring broccoli. No. Pickles of course.

Every day at lunch Oscar would say to Fuzzball, "You are my brother and my best friend. I love you but I will NEVER understand why you like the taste of horrible, yucky, gucky, stinky pickles." Then Fuzzball would say, "Oscar you are my brother and my best friend. I love you but I will NEVER understand why you like the horrible yucky, gucky, stinky taste of pizza and peanut butter, pitui, pitui, pitui!" And then everyone in Fuzzball's family would laugh and laugh because they knew that everyone is different and that sometimes things get complicated and that yelling and spinning on the floor always makes a complicated situation more complicated but laughing with your best friend makes everything better.

Songs

Some of these songs have been with me a long time. Over the years, people have asked me for chords and lyrics. I've included them along with some information about how and when they were written.

Rascal.

Back in the early 90s, I needed a song to start my show that would address all the obstacles that I felt were between me and the audience.

I was opening for a lot of bigger acts. Making fans out of an audience that came to see someone else is no easy feat. While you are singing, they are ordering and being served food. They came with their friends. They know they must be quiet while the headliner is on so they are likely to talk to each other during your set. Add to that the fact that some of the previous openers they saw were unimpressive, and you can see that the situation is not ideal for the kind of deep connection that makes fans out of people who don't know you. On the plus side, they may have low expectations.

I made a list of what I wanted my opening song to accomplish. I wrote "Rascal" specifically to demand attention. I wanted it to foreshadow in small doses all the fun we were going to have if they'd give me their attention.

It needed to show my sense of humor—that I was married with kids—my mischief and everything about me that might create the possibility in the minds of the folks in the audience that they might be on the verge of discovering an artist they could support in the future.

I tried to include as many of my performing tricks as possible— flirting, howling, and being the person in the room who was having the most fun.

The chords are a standard 1950s rock and roll progression.

Rascal

G   Em   C   D7
Rascal is the dog and he ain't too bright
Me and Rascal were sitting on the couch last night
When my woman come in and she started to cry
She looked at us with such terror in her eyes

She said, "I have raised these children for eighteen years
Now they're both growing up and moving out of here
And my big reward for all that I've been through
Is this dog as dumb—this dog as dumb as mud
This dog as dumb as mud and you"

Rascal looked at me in disbelief he said,
"She can't be talking about you and me
She's got us to spend the rest of her whole life with
Would you please tell her how incredibly lucky she is"

C
And I said, "Who's gonna love you any better than this
G
We'll wake you up every morning with them big wet kisses
C
When we hear the police sirens in your neighborhood
A   D7
We throw our heads up in the air and we howl for you
And that's cool
You gotta admit that's cool"

I don't believe that we'd succeeded in convincing her
Of the outrageous good fortune that had befallen her
In fact instead of looking happy as she could be
She looked a little bit, well you know, suicidal to me
But hey kids go to college and kids move away
Dogs and husbands that's who stay
To her it seems like a terrible trick of fate
But me and Rascal don't see it that way

We're thinking, ain't we cuddly ain't we cute
We're both real funny we're both real true
And there's another thing about us that is really cool
When you scratch us on our bellies our left leg moves
And you gotta admit that's cool

Okay so maybe we ain't that smart
Just a couple of mutts with a lotta heart
But no one could ever love you better or give you more loyalty
Than this dog as dumb as mud
This dog as dumb as mud
This dog as dumb as mud—and me
How lucky can one girl be?
She's got a dog like you and a man like me
We'll be together well into the next century

I Know What Love is

I thought this song was done after the verse about the grandparents. A couple of weeks later the last verse came to me while I was driving on the highway. I had to pull over and take a minute. It was very emotional.

This is a once-in-a-lifetime song for me. I couldn't possibly list all the fans and career opportunities that it has brought into my life.

The interesting thing to me is that I almost always write songs in a workmanlike manner. I know what I want to say and I think about how best to say it in song.

This song is the exception. It just sort of came to me and wouldn't leave me alone till I wrote it down.

I always sing it a cappella. So, no chords here.

I Know What Love Is

There is a little girl with pretty curls she's about five years old
And waiting at the gate for her dad to come home
When he pulls round the corner in his shiny white car
She feels the magic light up in her heart

He picks her up and he holds her
He says he missed her and he is glad that she is here
As the child lays her head on his shoulder
She whispers these words in his ear.

I know exactly what love is, love is real simple and true
Love is this feeling my heart gets
When I'm being held close by you

Now she is twenty and there is plenty of love everywhere
She is getting married so her family and her friend are all there
They have gathered this morning to stand at her side
As she waves goodbye to this time in her life

Then they each take a moment to hold her
And to tell her what she means to them
In a world that seems to keep getting colder
She has been blessed with a warm family and friends

I know exactly what love is, love is real simple and true
Love is this feeling my heart gets
When I'm being held close by you

Now they are older and no one told her it got crazy like this
They're going to night school they're working jobs too
And they are raising three kids
The youngest one is crying with a bruise on her knee
She needs attention and she needs sympathy

When she picks her up and she holds her
That old magic lights up in her heart
As that child lays her head on her shoulder
She knows exactly why they're working so hard

I know exactly what love is, love is real simple and true
Love is this feeling my heart gets
When I'm being held close by you

Now they are sixty and their history spans forty odd years
They have buried their parents now their grandkids are here
There is something about the way they look in each other's eyes
That speaks softly about the meaning of life

When he puts his arm out to hold her
It feels so familiar and warm
She thinks love is an expanding endeavor till your last breath
From the moment you're born

I know exactly what love is, love is real simple and true
Love is this feeling my heart gets
When I'm being held close by you

Now she is eighty and she hates being in this nursing home
Her man has been gone now for a long while
And she feels so alone
She closes her eyes and she begins to pray
That a little comfort might just come her way

Then God lifts her up and he holds her
And she remembers this feeling she has
She is not a woman whose life is almost over
She is a little girl being held by her dad

I know exactly what love is, love is real simple and true,
Love is this feeling my heart gets
When I'm being held close by you

Don White Copyright 1992
Lumperboy Music

Be Sixteen With Me

This one has no underlying message. I just thought it was funny to tell my wife that we should turn the tables on our adult children to make it as difficult as possible for them to keep living with us.

This song is always fun to play.
The chords are simple.
You can learn it in no time.

Be Sixteen with Me

G
Our kids are grown
G
They're both in their twenties
G
They live at home
G   D7
They are never gonna leave

D7
Why should they go
                    G
They've got it good here you know
        A
Their food, their phone, their rent is free
                D7
They would have to be outta their minds to leave

G
But I've been thinking
G
What if things were different
G   D7
Living here at home with you and me
D7
What if we decided we could act like
D7   G
They both did when they were in their teens

```
     G
So wake up mama
G
Climb out of this window
G
I've got the key
G                         D7
Let's steal our daughter's car
D7
We'll both get really drunk
G
We'll put a big dent in her trunk
       A
We'll drive real fast down the thoroughfare
D7
If we get a speeding ticket
D7
We won't care


G
We'll be the ones up all night acting wild
G                             D7
They'll be the ones up all night worrying
D7
Wake up Mama
D7
Climb out of this window
D7
Come on out
D7                  G
And be sixteen with me
```

Picture our kids calling
All our friends up
Asking them if they
Know where we are

Of course all our friends will lie
And say they ain't seen us all night

But we'll be standing right beside them
While they're on the phone
Smoking and drinking
And carrying on

And they'll be the ones
Trying to find the truth out
And we'll be the ones
Who are lying through our teeth

Under pressure we'll confess
That we had unprotected sex
That will gross them out so much
They might just
Start to think about moving out

If turnabout is fair play
In this life
What better way to encourage
Them to leave

Than to give them both a dose
Of what it was like
To live with them when they were in their teens

So wake up Mama
Climb out of this window
I've got the key
Let's steal our daughter's car

We'll both get really drunk
We'll put a big dent in her trunk
No one will know where we are
Till we come home in
A police car

Don White Copyright 2002
Lumperboy Music

The Painter

This is my wife's favorite song of mine.

Because it is yet another a cappella piece, I don't sing it as often as the others. When I wrote it, I was thinking about all the people I knew who were struggling with overwhelming challenges.

I was also thinking about the people who love these folks.

I was hoping that they remember to take care of themselves.

The Painter

This portrait of sadness
In the big gallery
Has a man in the foreground
In such misery
But the horizon behind him
Is vibrant and bright
We see him staring into darkness
But covered in light

If I were the painter
I'd paint you with wings
I would dress you in the colors
That come in the spring
When your heart was in darkness
And you were alone
I'd paint sunshine around you
And wings to carry you home

This portrait of anger
And low self-esteem
Shows a woman in danger
Of a life without dreams
And as I stare at her shoulders
Lord all I can see
Is this mountain of burden
Where wings ought to be

If I were the painter
I'd paint you with wings
I would dress you in the colors

That come in the spring
When your heart was in darkness
And you were alone
I'd paint sunshine around you
And wings to carry you home

This face in the mirror
This portrait of me
Is constantly changing
For the whole world to see
But the hand on the brushes
That color this face
Is the hand that belongs to
The person it paints

So if I am the painter
I will paint me with wings
And I will dress me in the colors
That come in the spring
And when my heart is in darkness
And I am alone
I will paint sunshine around me
And wings to carry me home

I will paint sunshine around me
And wings to carry me home

More Alive

I was at my mother's funeral. I was staring at the wall and thinking, "I'm not sure I'm made out of whatever you need to be made out of to live through this." I wasn't going to jump out of a window, but I was wrecked.

I looked across the room and saw my mother's friend. At the time she was eighty-two. She likes to dance and drink and pinch you on the butt and tell naughty jokes. She's the most dangerous eighty-two-year-old in the world and everyone wants to be near her because they know something memorable will happen.

I thought about how many loved ones she lost in her life. And how good she was at dealing with those losses and returning to life with more mischief and laughter after she was done mourning.

I wrote "More Alive" to remind myself that if I'm lucky enough to live to my eighties I want to be like her.

More Alive

```
          D                Bm
I lost my mother I lost my father
               Em
Well, I really didn't lose them
                    A
I know exactly where they both are
               D
It's not like they went for a walk
                    Bm
Took a wrong turn and both got lost
                Em
It just hurts less to say I lost them
A                 D
Than to say they're dead
```

Betty Mae is eighty-two
She's having more fun than me and you
All she wants to do is laugh and sing
She's the biggest flirt I ever seen
She still flutters those baby blues
Like she did when she was twenty-two
So much mischief in those eyes
Never seen someone more alive

```
G              D
More alive, more alive
       Em        G
Waiting on the other side
       Em                       A
Of all the sorrow and the trouble in your life
```

<pre>
        G   D
</pre>
There are so many sad goodbyes
<pre>
     Em   G
</pre>
In a long and well-lived life
<pre>
           Em   A
</pre>
If they don't break you, they can make you
<pre>
        D
</pre>
More alive

When my mother died
I was so smashed up inside
I was crying like a baby
I thought the pain might kill me

Betty said, "Son, you won't believe
How many loved ones I buried
My father, sister, my brother
My son, my husband, and my mother

Every time I lose a friend
I think I'm never gonna laugh again
I lay around and watch bad TV
Until this feeling comes over me

Then I put some music on
Play my favorite song
Dance around my living room
Like I did when I was twenty-two

I shake loose of that pain inside
On the day that I decide
Not only will I survive
But I am going to be more alive"

More alive, more alive
Waiting on the other side
Of all the sorrow and the trouble in your life
There are so many sad goodbyes
In a long and well-lived life
If they don't break you, they can make you
More alive

She said, "Go ahead feel your pain
Watch bad TV for days
But when you're ready to come out and play
You come see Betty Mae

We'll put some music on
Play your favorite song
Dance around my living room
Like we both were twenty-two

Shake loose of that pain inside
On the day that you decide
Not only will you survive
You're gonna be more alive"

More alive, more alive
Waiting on the other side
Of all the sorrow and the trouble in your life
There are so many sad goodbyes
In a long and well-lived life
If they don't break you, they can make you
More alive

There are so many sad goodbyes
In a long and well-lived life
If they don't break you
In time . . . they can make you more alive

Don White Copyright 2014
Lumperboy Music

Sassy Brat

When young people ask me how to know if a person they're dating at eighteen will be the one they can grow old with, I have no idea what to say. But that doesn't stop me from lying to them. I'll say anything. "The first things you need to look for in a possible soul mate are opposable thumbs. All old married people know that the key to a long relationship is to be able to turn the doorknob and get away from one another."

If they press me, I'll tell them that looking back I can see three things that really help. The first one is empathy. If you marry someone who is kind and can empathize—for me, that's a hard thing to fall out of love with. Next, see if they are strong under pressure. Over the course of a long relationship, you really want your partner to rise to the occasion during the rough times. But, the most important question is "Does he or she make you laugh?"

You simply cannot overstate the value of laughter over the course of a lifetime together.

Here's to all the sassy brats and the spouses lucky enough to have them.

Sassy Brat

G
In the forty years that we've been wed
                 C
I've wondered if you ever heard a word I said
           G
Till I said pass that remote control over here
        C
And you told me to blow it out my ear

  G
I love you you're a sassy brat
    C
You make me mad you make me laugh
G
God please don't cut our time in half
     C   G
Let me grow old with my sassy brat

When my fans call up and say that I'm great
You tell them that that is a huge mistake
If they had to live with me they would understand
What a big pain in the ass I am

I love you you're a sassy brat
You make me mad you make me laugh
God please don't cut our time in half
Let me grow old with my sassy brat

C
There are men who like women they can dominate
                  G
Who bring them breakfast in bed
G
And always tell them they're great
C
My sassy lady never does that for me
             D7
But at least life with her is definitely not boring

She says if you want me to believe that you're great
Do a couple loads of laundry around here someday
Hey pal, it's only because you're still kinda cute
That I haven't already gotten rid of you

I love you you're a sassy brat
You make me mad you make me laugh
God please don't cut our time in half
Let me grow old with my sassy brat

You say the kids have both gone to the show
How about a little quickie before they come home
I say that I suppose you think you're really slick
The way that you keep emphasizing little and quick

Sassy bratty lady has been hanging round here
Driving me crazy for all these years
If I could ever afford do see a psychiatrist
I'd ask him why the hell do I like being treated like this

We were in bed but we were still awake
You said I really love you and this life we've made
I said, "Can I quote you on what you just said?"
You told me if I did, you'd punch me in the head

I love you you're a sassy brat
You make me mad you make me laugh
God please don't cut our time in half
Let me grow old with my sassy brat

Don White Copyright 1994
Lumperboy Music

Angel in Pieces

As I recall, I had written the words to the chorus of what would later turn out to be "Angel in Pieces" on a scrap of paper and, as is the case more often than I care to tell, I forgot about it.

Months later I was doing a show with Jim Infantino and some other folks in Newburyport, Mass. It was cold in the dressing room and I told Jim that he was welcome to put on my sport jacket. He did so and pulled out the scrap of paper from the inside pocket. He said, "Don these are good lyrics. You should do something with them."

What eventually emerged was a song about believing in people when they're not well enough to believe in themselves.

Jon Svetkey wrote the music. The song works well with just guitar and vocal. It also can get really big when played with a band. It's a joy to sing.

Angel in Pieces

G
She walked into the room
          D
Like she was walking off a cliff
     Em
In my mind I said
              D
What kind of shattered angel is this
    G
Her walk said, I've surrendered
   D
Her face, I've had enough
Em
Her eyes were holes
Em
They were dark and cold
D
They said, I've given up

G   C
I saw an angel in pieces
Am   Bm   C D
As if the pieces all fell from the sky
G   F#m   B7
I said in my heart I believe this
Em   C   D
Sad angel someday will fly

Life rains down so hard upon
Some people that we know

It tears their faith and hope away
And they walk around like ghosts

We see them as they are breaking
And as their spirit dies
But deep inside we still believe
They will come alive and fly

I saw an angel in pieces
As if the pieces all fell from the sky
I said in my heart I believe this
Sad angel someday will fly

Now she walks across the room
Like she could walk across the sky
Those old dark eyes are so alive
They set the room on fire

This is no shattered angel
I say to myself
I feel Zuzu's petals
I hear one small bell

I saw an angel in pieces
As if the pieces all fell from the sky
I said in my heart I believe this
Sad angel someday will fly

Words Don White
Music Jon Svetkey
Copyright 1999
Lumperboy Music

That's What Makes You Beautiful

The final song here is the last one I wrote before devoting all my energy to writing this book. I have wanted to write this song for decades.

If you were raised by people who were, for whatever reason, not able to show you kindness or empathy or generosity but somehow you taught yourself how to acquire these qualities, I want you to know that I appreciate the miracle of what you have accomplished in your life.

That's What Makes You Beautiful

```
Bm              D
```
You were taught by your world
```
    Bm              D
```
That empathy and kindness were
```
    Bm                              A
```
The kinds of things that made a person weak
```
        Bm                  D
```
They said, "push and grab and fight
```
    Bm              D
```
Every minute of your life
```
    Bm                                          A
```
And trample those between you and what you believe you need"
```
        G                  D
```
But from the moment you were born
```
    G              D
```
In your heart there was a song
```
        Bm                              A
```
You could hear through all those years of fear and insecurity
```
        Bm              D
```
Singing, "cruelty is always weak
```
    Bm          D
```
But love and empathy
```
    Bm                              A7
```
Are strong enough to break the chains of selfishness and greed
```
G           A              D
```
Gentle is the strongest thing to be"

You know it is not your fault
That heroin and alcohol
Made them both too ill to give their children
What they really need

But it sure would have been nice
To be encouraged once or twice
To feel safe at night or to have a life with just a little normalcy

But from the moment you were born
In your heart there was a song
You could hear through all those years of fear and insecurity

"When you feel hatred in your heart
Just remember who you are
And that underneath the weight of hate your heart cannot be free
Forgiving is the stronger thing to be"

```
G                         D
It's not the color of your eyes
          G           D
It's not your hypnotizing smile
     Bm                          F#m         A
It's not any of the many things that everyone can see
     Bm              D
It's the way you always knew
          Bm          D
What they told you wasn't true
             Bm
It's how you made yourself the person
```

                A7
That they taught you not to be
G   A   D
That's what makes you beautiful to me

A young man's eyes see beauty in
What is on the surface, not within
He will walk past what is beautiful
To be near the thing that shines

But these old man's eyes see beauty
In the story, in the journey
They have seen too much to be fooled
By what attracts a young man's eyes

From the moment you were born
In your heart there was a song
You could hear through all those years
Of fear and insecurity

There was nothing that this world could do
To crush the love inside of you
Under neglect, abuse and selfishness
You were caring, kind and generous

```
G                         D
It is the lonely road that brought you here
         G          D
It's how all alone you persevered
         G          D
It's the defiance and tenacity


         A7
Of your heart song of humanity
G                    A
That's what makes you beautiful
G                    A
That's what makes you beautiful
G                    A
That's what makes you beautiful
     D
To me
```

Words: Don White
Music: Don White & Hayley Reardon
Copyright 2020
Lumperboy Music

www.DonWhite.net